natural knits
for Babies and Mums

natural knits
for Babies and Mums

Beautiful Designs Using
Organic Yarns

LOUISA
HARDING

SEARCH PRESS

NATURAL KNITS FOR BABIES AND MOMS
originally published in America 2006 by:
Interweave Press LLC
201 East Fourth Street
Loveland, CO 80537-5655 USA
www.interweave.com

Retitled NATURAL KNITS FOR BABIES AND MUMS
and first published in Great Britain 2006 by:
Search Press Ltd
Wellwood
North Farm Road
Tunbridge Wells
Kent TN2 3DR

Text © 2006 by Louisa Harding
Photography © 2006 by Stephen Jessup

ISBN 978-1-84448-202-3

Editor: Anne Merrow
Technical editor: Karen Frisa
Photography: Stephen Jessup
Photo styling: Louisa Harding
Cover and interior design: Paulette Livers
Illustrations: Louisa Harding
Production: Paulette Livers
Copy editor: Cari Luna
Proofreader and indexer: Nancy Arndt

SUPPLIERS
If you have any difficulty obtaining any of the materials and equipment
mentioned in this book, then please visit the Search Press website for details
of suppliers:
www.searchpress.com.

Printed in China by C&C Offset Printing Co. Ltd.

10 9 8 7 6 5 4 3 2 1

Always for Belle and Oscar
Thankfully, children change everything.

Acknowledgments

This book would not be possible without the help of the following people: Stephen Jessup, my rock; Granny Daph, Nana Carole, and Auntie Di Di; and my wonderful knitters: Betty Rothwell, Mrs. Marsh, Daphne Harding, Mary Butler, Beryl White, Mrs. Wilmot, and Janet Mann. Thank you to our wonderful models: our expectant mother, Rachel Lyne, who gave birth to Jasmine Elia on November 11, 2005; the gorgeous girls: Claire and Kitty, Sarah, Amelie, Holly, and Daisy; the very handsome boys: Tommy, Kai, and Geordie; and their mums, whose kisses and cuddles have made these pictures so intimate and beautiful.

Finally, thank you to Betsy Armstrong and the team at Interweave Press for their encouragement and for enabling this exciting book to happen.

CONTENTS

Introduction

Pregnancy and the birth of a new baby are exciting times for everyone involved, whether you are an expectant mother, new parent, grandparent, auntie, uncle, or simply a good friend.

It is often a time of contemplation, when you examine your life and wonder how to introduce this new being to its surroundings. When I was pregnant, I wanted my choices to have a positive impact on my new babies. I asked myself questions regarding their upbringing—How would I raise them? What kind of environment did I want to provide for them?—as well as how I could combine my creative life with having young children.

Thankfully, children change everything. For me and my husband, Stephen, they released a creative energy that had previously lain dormant. Wanting to be at home with the children and be inspired by them, I began designing hand knitwear patterns for children and eventually created a book, *Miss Bea's Playtime*. My husband took very naturalistic photos and designed the layouts to appeal to new, returning, and more accomplished knitters, and the Miss Bea series was the result.

Then, on a visit to America, I was inspired by the spinners who were producing organic yarns. I had not realized that such a wide range of organically and naturally produced yarns were available, and their abundance fueled an idea: I wanted to combine my designs, these amazing yarns, and my husband's photography in order to reflect my philosophy of new life and new babies: keeping them wrapped in as natural an environment as possible, just like the one they've come from.

This book is the outcome of those ideas and inspirations, a beautifully photographed collection of twenty-one handknit designs using organically grown yarns. It is designed to provide a collection of handknitted items that are perfect for mother and baby's first eighteen months— from pregnancy attire to a going-home set, tiny booties to chunky jackets, cot blankets to cleverly conceived pillows and toys stuffed with sleep-inducing and calming herbs. I hope this book will awaken your creative energy, whether you are knitting for yourself or a new mother or baby in your life. The projects here will envelop those most precious to you, and with every knitted stitch you'll pass on love and affection.

Make a Gift of Your Knitting

Many of the designs in the book were planned as gift ideas. A new baby is a great incentive to begin knitting, or it can act as the catalyst to return to the craft. I have included very easy patterns that are ideal for the novice knitter, such as the super-easy Blanket and Hat and the Cat, Rabbit, and Teddy Bear toys. More traditional gift ideas include the hats and booties ensembles.

I designed the multicolored square Cot Blanket with the idea that a group of friends, family members, or a knitting group could make the project together, with each knitter making a square in a different color. When all the squares are completed, they can then be sewn together and presented at a baby shower, a beautiful way of showing your love and creating an heirloom to pass on for many generations.

A Note on Sizes

The sizes for each garment are given at the beginning of every pattern. The ages are listed only as a guide. As babies vary, make sure you choose the right garment size—measure an item of the baby's clothing that fits well and choose the pattern size that matches. If you're still unsure, knit a larger size, as babies always grow.

Yarn Information

Each of the yarns used in this book is made from organic cotton or wool. You can purchase these yarns in person at the yarn store or from across the world using the Internet. In the yarn store, you will find helpful, knowledgeable staff and an amazing array of products including knitting yarns, needles, buttons, and books. There are also many good on-line yarn suppliers, which are a fantastic resource of information; you can see the whole spectrum of colors in yarn ranges and order shade cards to help you get a feel for the yarns available. However, when you first begin to knit, visit a yarn store first if possible, both to get an idea of what they have to offer and to feel the balls of yarn. You will find a marvelous array of color and texture—the selection is unbelievable, and you will feel like a child in a sweet shop.

Organic wool is produced from the fleece of animals reared on organically farmed, pesticide-free land. The yarns are washed and spun using vegetable-based soaps and oils; no chemicals are used to bleach or treat the yarn. Many of the organic wool yarns used here are spun using un-dyed fleece, which gets its color from the natural shade of the sheep. Color variations can be achieved by spinning or plying different natural colors together.

Traditional wool yarn can be too itchy to wear close to the skin, but many spinners now make very soft wool blends using different types of fleece. If you use a wool yarn that is slightly coarse in texture, I suggest handwashing the finished pieces with environmentally friendly wool wash, which will make the fabric feel wonderfully soft.

Organic cotton is grown and harvested without the use of agrochemicals. The colors in the organic cottons used in this book are grown that way—the yarns have been bred so that the intensity of color comes from the cotton bud itself. As you might expect, the cottons have very earthy tones, ranging from very pale naturals to beige and brown and even sage and dark green. The yarn is soft and feels nice against the skin, but it does not have much elasticity. It can also be quite heavy, so it is not practical for big garments or blankets.

Wool and cotton mix is a good compromise, as it has the softness of cotton but retains heat and elasticity like pure wool. The wool/cotton blends used in this book have been dyed using environmentally friendly processes.

Substituting Yarns

I have designed the projects in this book using specific yarns for their organic qualities as well as their knitting properties. You may wish to substitute the yarn of your choice but please take care if you do this; each pattern has been worked out mathematically to produce the specified sizes. If you use a different yarn, look for a similar yarn with the same gauge and yardage stated on the label and knit a swatch of your chosen yarn before embarking on the pattern. You must achieve the pattern's stated gauge, or your project will turn out too big or too small.

Cautions aside, it can be fun to substitute yarns—it may start you thinking creatively about knitting.

Bump Sweater

This pattern is so simple, but the idea behind it is really innovative: short row shaping on the front provides extra room to accommodate a growing bump. The ribbon ties are decorative but also practical—let them out as needed.

To fit bust circumference			
33½–35½	37½–39½	41½–43½	45½–47½"
85–90	95–100.5	105.5–110.5	115.5–120.5 cm
Finished bust circumference			
39½	43½	47½	51½"
100.5	110.5	120.5	131 cm
Actual width at underarm			
19¾	21¾	23¾	25¾"
50	55	60.5	65.5 cm
Armhole depth			
8	8	8	8"
20.5	20.5	20.5	20.5 cm
Neck width			
9½	9½	9½	9½"
24	24	24	24 cm
Finished length			
21¼	22¼	23¼	24¼"
54	56.5	59	61.5 cm
Sleeve length			
15¼	15¼	15¼	15¼"
38.5	38.5	38.5	38.5 cm
Sleeve width			
15	15	15	15"
38	38	38	38 cm

Yarn

Worsted weight (CYCA Medium #4): 790 (840, 925, 1005) yd (722 [768, 846, 919] m).

Shown here: Blue Sky Alpacas Organic Cotton (100% organic cotton; 150 yd [137 m]/100 g): #80 bone, 6 (6, 7, 7) balls. Sweater shown measures 43½" (110.5 cm).

Needles

U.S. 8 (5 mm): straight. Adjust needle size if necessary to obtain the correct gauge.

Notions

Tapestry needle; two ½" (1.25-cm) wide pieces of ribbon, each 48" (122 cm) long.

Gauge

16 sts and 22 rows = 4" (10 cm) in St st.

Notes

The front and back of the sweater are knitted from side to side, beginning at the left side seam for the back and the right side seam for the front. The sleeves are knitted from underarm to underarm.

Back

CO 85 (89, 93, 97) sts.

Left vent edging

Row 1: (RS) [K1, p1] 25 times, k25 (29, 33, 37), [p1, k1] 5 times.

Row 2: [K1, p1] 5 times, p26 (30, 34, 38), [k1, p1] 24 times, k1.

Row 3: [K1, p1] 24 times, k27 (31, 35, 39), [p1, k1] 5 times.

Row 4: [K1, p1] 5 times, p28 (32, 36, 40), [k1, p1] 23 times, k1.

Row 5: (eyelet row) K1, p1, [yo, p2tog, (k1, p1) twice] 7 times, k1, p1, k29 (33, 37, 41), [p1, k1] 5 times.

Row 6: [K1, p1] 5 times, p30 (34, 38, 42), [k1, p1] 22 times, k1.

Row 7: [K1, p1) 22 times, k31 (35, 39, 43), [p1, k1] 5 times.

Row 8: [K1, p1] 5 times, p32 (36, 40, 44), [k1, p1] 21 times, k1.

Row 9: [K1, p1] 21 times, k33 (37, 41, 45), [p1, k1] 5 times.

Row 10: [K1, p1] 5 times, p34 (38, 42, 46), [k1, p1] 20 times, k1.

Body

Row 11: [K1, p1] 5 times, k65 (69, 73, 77), [p1, k1] 5 times.

Row 12: [K1, p1] 5 times, p66 (70, 74, 78), [k1, p1] 4 times, k1.

Rep Rows 11 and 12 until piece measures 18 (20, 22, 24)" (45.5 [51, 56, 61] cm) from CO, ending with a RS row.

Right vent edging

Row 1: (WS) [K1, p1] 5 times, p34 (38, 42, 46), [k1, p1] 20 times, k1.

Row 2: [K1, p1] 21 times, k33 (37, 41, 45), [p1, k1] 5 times.

Row 3: [K1, p1] 5 times, p32 (36, 40, 44), [k1, p1] 21 times, k1.

Row 4: [K1, p1] 22 times, p31 (35, 39, 43), [p1, k1] 5 times.

Row 5: [K1, p1] 5 times, p30 (34, 38, 42), [k1, p1] 22 times, k1.

Row 6: (RS, eyelet row) K1, p1, [yo, p2tog, (k1, p1) twice] 7 times, k1, p1, k29 (33, 37, 41), [p1, k1] 5 times.

Row 7: [K1, p1] 5 times, p28 (32, 36, 40), [k1, p1] 23 times, k1.

Row 8: [K1, p1] 24 times, k27 (31, 35, 39), [p1, k1] 5 times.

Row 9: [K1, p1] 5 times, p26 (30, 34, 38), [k1, p1] 24 times, k1.

Row 10: (RS) [K1, p1] 25 times, k25 (29, 33, 37), [p1, k1] 5 times.

BO all sts knitwise.

Front

CO 85 (89, 93, 97) sts. Work left vent edging as for back.

Body

Row 11: [K1, p1] 5 times, k65 (69, 73, 77), [p1, k1] 5 times.

Row 12: [K1, p1] 5 times, p66 (70, 74, 78), [k1, p1] 4 times, k1.

Rep last 2 rows 1 (4, 7, 10) more time(s).

Shape bump

Work short-rows (see Glossary, page 124) as foll:

*Row 1: (RS) [K1, p1] 5 times, k65 (69, 73, 77), wrap next st and turn (w & t).

Row 2: (WS) P66 (70, 74, 78), [k1, p1] 4 times, k1.

Row 3: [K1, p1] 5 times, k65 (69, 73, 77), [p1, k1] 5 times.

Row 4: [K1, p1] 5 times, p66 (70, 74, 78), [k1, p1] 4 times, k1.

Rows 5–12: Rep Rows 3–4 four more times. Rep from * 8 more times.

Next row: (RS) [K1, p1] 5 times, k65 (69, 73, 77), [p1, k1] 5 times.

Next row: [K1, p1] 5 times, p66 (70, 74, 78), [k1, p1] 4 times, k1.

Rep last 2 rows 1 (4, 7, 10) more time(s), ending with a WS row.

Next row: (RS) [K1, p1] 5 times, k65 (69, 73, 77), [p1, k1] 5 times.

Work right vent edging as for back. BO all sts knitwise.

Sleeves

CO 61 sts.

Row 1: (RS) [K1, p1] 5 times, k51.

Row 2: P52, [k1, p1] 4 times, k1.

Rep Rows 1 and 2 for pattern. Work even until piece measures 15" (38 cm) from CO, ending with a RS row. BO all sts knitwise.

Finishing

Block pieces to measurements. With yarn threaded on a tapestry needle, sew shoulder seams, leaving 9½" (24 cm) open for neck. Place markers along side edges of front and back 8" (20.5 cm) below shoulder seams to mark sleeve placement. Place sleeve between markers, matching center of sleeve to shoulder seam. Sew sleeves to back and front between markers. Sew side seams from underarm to top of vent edging, leaving seed st vent open. Sew sleeve seams. Weave in loose ends. Block again if desired. Lace ribbon through eyelets in seed st vent.

Cot Blanket

This project makes a great baby shower present and a fabulous way to show mother and new baby how much they are treasured. Each square is knitted separately and then sewn together. Get together with a group of friends or relatives and make this blanket as a group gift.

Yarn
DK weight (CYCA Light #3): about 135 yd (123 m) in each of 6 colors.
Shown here: Green Mountain Spinnery Cotton Comfort (20% organic cotton, 80% fine wool; 180 yd [165 m]/2 oz): #6-MI mint (light green), #6-D denim (dark blue), #6-PL pink lilac, #6-V violet, #6-B bluet (light blue), #6-WG weathered green (dark green), 1 skein each.
Needles
U.S. sizes 5 and 6 (3.75 and 4 mm): straight. Adjust needle size if necessary to obtain the correct gauge.
Notions
Tapestry needle.
Gauge
22 sts and 30 rows = 4" (10 cm) in St st on larger needles. Each square measures about 6³⁄₄" (17 cm) wide and 6½" (16.5 cm) long.

Finished Size
22¼" (56.5 cm) wide and 28" (71 cm) long.

Blanket

Seven Hearts Square (make 2)

With mint and larger needles, CO 37 sts.
Work Rows 1–49 of Seven Hearts chart. With WS facing, BO all sts knitwise.

Plaid Square (make 2)

With denim and larger needles, CO 37 sts.
Work Rows 1–49 of Plaid chart. With WS facing, BO all sts knitwise.

Three Hearts Square (make 2)

With pink lilac and larger needles, CO 37 sts.
Work Rows 1–49 of Three Hearts chart. With WS facing, BO all sts knitwise.

One Heart Square (make 2)

With violet and larger needles, CO 37 sts.
Work Rows 1–49 of One Heart chart. With WS facing, BO all sts knitwise.

Plain Square (make 2)

With bluet and larger needles, CO 37 sts.
Work Rows 1–49 of Plain chart. With WS facing, BO all sts knitwise.

Star Square (make 2)

With weathered green and larger needles, CO 37 sts.
Work Rows 1–49 of Star chart. With WS facing, BO all sts knitwise.

Finishing

Block squares to measurements. Arrange squares as shown in illustration on page 19. With yarn to match one of the squares being seamed threaded on a tapestry needle, whipstitch (see Glossary, page 123) squares together in 3 columns of 4 squares each. Sew columns together using edge-to-edge stitch (see Glossary, page 123).

Right side edging

With mint, smaller needles, and RS facing, pick up and knit 140 sts from bottom right corner to top right corner. Knit 1 row. Working in garter st, knit 2 rows each in denim, pink lilac, violet, and bluet. Knit 1 row in weathered green. With WS facing, BO all sts knitwise.

Left side edging

With denim, smaller needles, and RS facing, pick up and knit 140 sts from top left corner to bottom left corner. Knit 1 row.
Working in garter st, knit 2 rows each in pink lilac, violet, bluet, and weathered green, then knit 1 row in mint. With WS facing, BO all sts knitwise.

Top edging

With violet, smaller needles, and RS facing, pick up and knit 8 sts from right side edging, 110 sts from top edge, and 8 sts from left side edging—126 sts total. Knit 1 row.
Working in garter st, knit 2 rows each in bluet, weathered green, mint, and denim, then knit 1 row in pink lilac. With WS facing, BO all sts knitwise.

Bottom edging

With pink lilac, smaller needles, and RS facing, pick up and knit 8 sts from right side edging, 110 sts from lower edge, and 8 sts from left side edging—126 sts total. Knit 1 row. Working in garter st, knit 2 rows each of violet, bluet, weathered green, and mint, then knit 1 row in denim. With WS facing, BO all sts knitwise.

Weave in loose ends. Block again if desired.

One Heart

Plaid

Plain

Seven Hearts

Star

Three Hearts

☐ k on RS, p on WS

⊡ p on RS, k on WS

Textured Pillow

In this very simple design, the squares are knitted separately and sewn together to make an envelope-style pillow. You may wish to add a sachet of herbs to the pillow stuffing to make a relaxing herbal treat for an expecting or breast-feeding mother.

Yarn

Worsted weight (CYCA Medium #4): about 140 yd (128 m) in each of 4 colors.

Shown here: Blue Sky Alpacas Organic Cotton (100% organic cotton; 150 yd [137 m]/100 g): #81 sand (light tan), #83 sage, #80 bone (ivory), #82 nut (brown), 1 ball each.

Needles

U.S. sizes 7 and 8 (4.5 and 5 mm): straight. Adjust needle size if necessary to obtain the correct gauge.

Notions

Tapestry needle; seven ³/₄" (2-cm) buttons, shown here in mother-of-pearl; 18" (45.5-cm) square pillow form; sachet of dried herbs or a few drops of essential oils (optional).

Gauge

16 sts and 22 rows = 4" (10 cm) in St st on larger needles. Each square on pillow front measures about 9" (23 cm) wide and 9" (23 cm) long.

Stitch Guide

Seed stitch: (odd number of sts)

Row 1: *K1, p1; rep from * to last st, k1.

Rep Row 1 for pattern.

Finished Size
18" (45.5 cm) wide and 18" (45.5 cm) long.

Front   Back

Pillow Front

Plaid Square

With sand and larger needles, CO 37 sts. Work Rows 1–49 of Plaid chart. With WS facing, BO all sts knitwise.

Three Hearts Square

With sage and larger needles, CO 37 sts. Work Rows

1–49 of Three Hearts chart. With WS facing, BO all sts knitwise.

One Heart Square

With bone and larger needles, CO 37 sts. Work Rows 1–49 of One Heart chart. With WS facing, BO all sts knitwise.

Star Square

With nut and larger needles, CO 37 sts. Work Rows 1–49 of Star chart. With WS facing, BO all sts knitwise.

Pillow Back

Plaid Square

With sand and larger needles, CO 37 sts. Work Rows 1–49 of Plaid Square chart.

Buttonhole edging

Work 1 row in seed st (see Stitch Guide).

Next row: (RS; buttonhole) Work 6 sts in seed st, [yo, p2tog, work 10 sts in seed st] twice, yo, p2tog, work 5 sts in seed st.

Work 2 more rows in seed st.

With WS facing, BO all sts knitwise.

Star Square

With nut and larger needles, CO 37 sts. Work Rows 1–49 of Star chart.

Buttonhole edging

Work 1 row in seed st.

Next row: (RS; buttonhole) Work 6 sts in seed st, [yo, p2tog, work 10 sts in seed st] twice, yo, p2tog, work 5 sts in seed st.

Work 2 more rows in seed st.

With WS facing, BO all sts knitwise.

Three Hearts Square

With sage and larger needles, CO 37 sts. Work 6 rows in seed st for button band, then work Rows 1–49 of Three Hearts chart. With WS facing, BO all sts knitwise.

One Heart Square

With bone and larger needles, CO 37 sts. Work 6 rows in seed st for button band, then work Rows 1–49 of One Heart chart. With WS facing, BO all sts knitwise.

Finishing

Block squares to measurements.

Arrange squares for front and back as shown in the illustrations on page 23. With yarn to match one of the squares being seamed threaded on a tapestry needle, backstitch (see Glossary, page 123) squares for front together. Backstitch squares for upper back together, then squares for lower back. Backstitch upper back to top and sides of front, leaving button band unsewn at each side. Backstitch lower back to bottom and sides of front, overlapping buttonhole edging over button band, and backstitching front, upper back, and lower back together at button band. Sew 6 buttons onto button band to correspond with buttonholes. Sew 1 button to center of right side of pillow. Weave in loose ends. Insert pillow form. Insert herb sachet or essential oils if desired.

Beanie Hat

So simple and quick to knit, this hat takes only a few hours to complete.
The boy's hat has funky stripes, while the girl's features lazy daisy embroidery.
Together with the booties (page 29) and mittens (page 32), these make a
lovely gift set.

To fit ages		
up to 3 mos.	up to 6 mos.	up to 12 mos.
Finished circumference		
13¾	15¼	16¾"
35	38.5	42.5 cm

Yarn

DK weight (CYCA Light #3): about 40 (50, 60) yd
(37 [46, 55] m), plus a few yd CC for embroidery
for girl's beanie.

Shown here: Cottage Industry Pakucho (100%
organic cotton; 95 yd [87 m]/1.75 oz): girl's beanie,
#2 vanilla (MC), 1 ball, #6 avocado (CC), few yd (all
sizes); boy's striped beanie, #1 natural (MC), and
#5 chocolate (CC), 1 ball (all sizes). Hats shown
measure 13¾" (35 cm).

Needles

U.S. sizes 5 and 7 (3.75 and 4.5 mm): straight.
Adjust needle size if necessary to obtain the
correct gauge.

Notions

Tapestry needle.

Gauge

21 sts and 29 rows = 4" (10 cm) in St st on larger
needles.

Stitch Guide

Picot edge: Using the cable method (see Glossary,
page 119), *CO 5 sts, BO 2 sts, slip st on right needle
to left needle; rep from *—3 sts CO for each rep.

Girl's Beanie

With MC and smaller needles, work picot edge (see Stitch Guide) until there are 72 (78, 87) sts on needle, then CO 0 (2, 1) more st(s)—72 (80, 88) sts total.

Work 4 rows in garter st, ending with a WS row. Change to larger needles.

Body

Beg with a knit row, work 14 (16, 18) rows in St st, ending with a WS row.

Shape crown

Row 1: (RS; dec row) *K2tog, k7 (8, 9); rep from * to end—64 (72, 80) sts rem.

Rows 2–4: Beg with a purl row, work 3 rows in St st.

Row 5: *K2tog, k6 (7, 8); rep from * to end—56 (64, 72) sts rem.

Row 6 and all WS rows: Purl.

Row 7: *K2tog, k5 (6, 7); rep from * to end—48 (56, 64) sts rem.

Row 9: *K2tog, k4 (5, 6); rep from * to end—40 (48, 56) sts rem.

Cont to dec every RS row 3 (4, 5) more times as above, working 1 fewer st between decs on each dec row, ending with a RS row—16 sts rem.

Last row: (WS) *P2tog; rep from * to end—8 sts rem.

Cut yarn, leaving a 12" (30.5-cm) tail. Thread tail through rem sts, pull tight to gather sts, and fasten off on inside. Sew hat seam. Weave in loose ends. With CC, work lazy daisy embroidery (see Glossary, page 120) around the base of the hat as illustrated in the photograph.

Boy's Striped Beanie

With MC and smaller needles, CO 72 (80, 88) sts. Work in rib as foll:

Row 1: (RS) K1, *k2, p2; rep from * to last 3 sts, k3.

Row 2: K1, *p2, k2; rep from * to last 3 sts, p2, k1.

Rep Rows 1 and 2 once more, ending with a WS row.

Change to CC and larger needles. Working in striped St st of 2 rows CC, 2 rows MC throughout, work body and crown as for girl's beanie, omitting embroidery.

Boy's and Girl's Booties

I love to see handknitted booties worn on a pair of chubby baby legs. Watching babies' feet move furiously is a secret delight. Just like the delight babies show as they find their own feet, remove their booties and expose their toes.

To fit up to 3 mos.		
Length from heel to toe	3¾"	9.5 cm

Yarn
DK weight (CYCA Light #3): about 65 yd (59 m) MC plus about 5 yd (5 m) for twisted cord for boy's booties, and a few yd CC for embroidery for girl's booties.
Shown here: Cottage Industry Pakucho (100% organic cotton, 95 yd [87 m]/50 g): girl's booties, #6 avocado (MC), 1 ball, #2 vanilla (CC), few yd; boy's booties, #5 chocolate, 1 ball.

Needles
U.S. size 6 (4 mm): straight, and U.S. size 5 (3.75 mm): straight (for girl's booties only). Adjust needle size if necessary to obtain the correct gauge.

Notions
Stitch holders; tapestry needle; two ⅜" (1-cm) wide x 18" (45.5-cm) lengths of ribbon for girl's booties.

Gauge
22 sts and 30 rows = 4" (10 cm) in St st on larger needles.

Girl's Booties
With MC and smaller needles, CO 26 sts.
Row 1: (RS) *K2, p2; rep from * to last 2 sts, k2.
Row 2: (inc row) *P2, k2; rep from * to last 2 sts, p1, p1f&b—27 sts.
Change to larger needles and, beg with a knit row, work 9 rows in St st.
Next row: (WS; eyelet row) P3, *yo, p2tog, p1; rep from * to end.

Shape instep

Row 1: (RS) K18, turn. Place rem 9 sts on a holder for left ankle.

Row 2: P9, turn. Place rem 9 sts on a holder for right ankle.

Beg with a knit row, work 12 more rows in St st on these 9 sts for instep. Cut yarn. Place 9 sts on a holder for instep.

Shape foot

With larger needles and RS facing, rejoin yarn at beg of right ankle sts. K9 held right ankle sts, pick up and knit 9 sts along side of instep, k9 held sts of instep, pick up and knit 9 sts along other side of instep, k9 held left ankle sts—45 sts total.

Beg with a purl row, work 6 rows in St st.

Shape sole

Rows 1, 3, and 5: (WS) Knit.

Row 2: (RS; dec row) K2tog, k17, k2tog, k3, k2tog through back loop (tbl), knit to last 2 sts, k2tog tbl—41 sts rem.

Row 4: (dec row) K2tog, k16, k2tog, k1, k2tog tbl, knit to last 2 sts, k2tog tbl—37 sts rem.

Row 6: (dec row) K2tog, k15, sl1, k2tog, psso, knit to last 2 sts, k2tog tbl—33 sts rem.

With WS facing, BO all sts knitwise.

Boy's Booties

With larger needles, CO 26 sts.

Row 1: (RS) *K2, p2; rep from * to last 2 sts, k2.

Row 2: *P2, k2; rep from * to last 2 sts, p2.

Rows 3–10: Rep Rows 1 and 2 four more times.

Row 11: (inc row) *K2, p2; rep from * to last 2 sts, k1, k1f&b—27 sts.

Row 12: (WS; eyelet row) P3, *yo, p2tog, p1; rep from * to end.

Complete as for girl's booties, beg with instep shaping.

Finishing

Fold bootie in half with RS tog. With yarn threaded on a tapestry needle, sew sole and back seam.

Girl's Booties

With CC, work lazy daisy embroidery (see Glossary, page 120) as shown in the photograph. Thread ribbon through eyelets and secure with a bow.

Boy's Booties

Make two 18" (45.5-cm) lengths of twisted cord (see Glossary, page 121), using two 38" (96.5-cm) lengths of yarn for each. Thread twisted cord through eyelets and secure with a bow.

Mittens

Mittens are a lovely and useful project to knit. In my experience, however, getting a baby to keep mittens on her hands is a real challenge. I have a drawer full of single mittens, which is why I suggest joining the pair with a twisted cord for older babies.

To fit ages		
up to 3 mos.	up to 6 mos.	up to 12 mos.
Hand circumference		
5¼	6	6¾"
13.5	15	17 cm

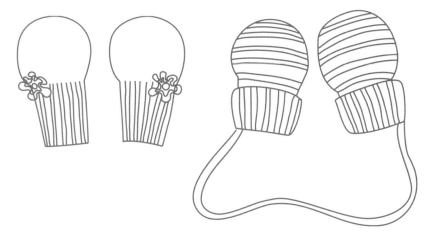

Yarn
DK weight (CYCA Light #3): about 85 (105, 145) yd (78 [96, 133] m) for solid mittens; 50 (60, 85) yd (46 [55, 78] m) MC and 35 (45, 60) yd (32 [41, 55] m) CC for striped mittens; plus 4 yd (4 m) for twisted cord on largest size.
Shown here: Green Mountain Spinnery Cotton Comfort (20% organic cotton, 80% fine wool; 180 yd [165 m]/2 oz): striped mittens, #6-UW unbleached white (MC) and #6-D denim (CC), 1 skein each; solid mittens, #6-PL pink lilac, 1 skein. Mittens shown measure 5¼" (13.5 cm).
Needles
U.S. sizes 3 and 6 (3.25 and 4 mm): straight. Adjust needle size if necessary to obtain the correct gauge.
Notions
Tapestry needle.
Gauge
22 sts and 30 rows = 4" (10 cm) in St st on larger needles.

Stitch Guide

Rib pattern: [multiple of 4 sts + 2 (0, 2)]

Row 1: (RS) P0 (1, 0), *[k2, p2]; rep from * to last 2 (3, 2) sts, k2, p0 (1, 0).

Row 2: K0 (1, 0), *[p2, k2]; rep from * to last 2 (3, 2) sts, p2, k0 (1, 0).

Rep Rows 1 and 2 for pattern.

Striped stockinette stitch:

Row 1: (RS) Knit with CC.

Row 2: Purl with CC.

Row 3: Knit with MC.

Row 4: Purl with MC.

Rep Rows 1–4 for pattern.

Striped Mittens

MC and smaller needles, CO 26 (28, 30) sts.

Work in rib pattern (see Stitch Guide) for 17 (19, 21) rows, ending with a RS row.

Next row: (WS; inc row) Work 1 (2, 3) st(s) in rib patt, [work 6 (4, 3) sts in rib patt, M1 (see Glossary, page 122)] 3 (5, 7) times, work 7 (6, 6) sts in rib patt—29 (33, 37) sts.

Change to CC and larger needles. Work in striped St st (see Stitch Guide) for 12 (14, 18) rows.

Shape top

Note: Cont in striped St st to end of mitten.

Row 1: (RS; dec row) K3tog tbl, k8 (10, 12), k3tog, k1, k3tog tbl, k8 (10, 12), k3tog—21 (25, 29) sts rem.

Row 2: Purl.

Row 3: (dec row) K3tog tbl, k4 (6, 8), k3tog, k1, k3tog tbl, k4 (6, 8), k3tog—13 (17, 21) sts rem.

6³/₄" (17 cm) size only

Row 4: Purl.

Row 5: (dec row) K3tog tbl, k4, k3tog, k1, k3tog tbl, k4, k3tog—13 sts rem.

All sizes

Cut yarn, leaving a 12" (30.5-cm) tail. Thread tail through rem sts, pull tight to gather sts, and fasten off on inside. Sew seam. Weave in loose ends.

Plain Mittens

Work as for striped mittens, working in one color throughout.

Decorate plain mitten with a flower at cuff if desired.

Flower

With larger needles, CO 36 sts.

K1, BO 4 sts (2 sts on right needle), *k1, BO 4 sts; rep from * to end—12 sts rem.

Cut yarn, leaving a 12" (30.5-cm) tail. Thread tail through rem sts, pull tight to gather sts, and fasten off on WS. With yarn threaded on a tapestry needle, sew flower into place.

Finishing

Cord for 6³/₄" (17 cm) size only

Make one 26" (66-cm) length of twisted cord (see Glossary, page 121), using two 54" (137-cm) lengths of yarn. Join mittens together by sewing each end of twisted cord to inside of cuffs.

Cat, Rabbit, and Teddy Bear

This really is the easiest pattern ever written for a knitted toy animal, but once you assemble the simple knitted rectangles and add distinguishing features, it will become a favorite member of the family. In our house, we have Mr. Pickles the Teddy, Sparks the Cat, and Florence the Rabbit, each with a huge personality of its own.

Yarn

Cat: DK weight (CYCA Light #3): about 80 yd (73 m) MC and 55 yd (50 m) CC.
Cat shown here: Green Mountain Spinnery Cotton Comfort (20% organic cotton, 80% fine wool; 180 yd [165 m]/2 oz): #6-S silver (MC) and #6-SM storm (dark grey, CC), 1 skein each.
Rabbit: Worsted weight (CYCA Medium #4): about 75 yd (69 m) MC, 40 yd (37 m) CC, and 1–2 yd (1–2 m) of a second contrasting color for embroidery on face.
Rabbit shown here: Blue Sky Alpacas Organic Cotton (100% organic cotton; 150 yd [137 m]/100 g): #82 nut (brown, MC), 1 ball; #81 sand (light tan, CC), 1 ball; dark brown wool yarn, 1–2 yd (1–2 m) for embroidery on face.
Teddy Bear: Worsted weight (CYCA Medium #4): about 95 yd (87 m) MC and 10 yd (9 m) CC.
Teddy Bear shown here: Vreseis Fox Fibre Chenille (100% cotton; 1000 yd [914 m]/1 lb): brown (MC), less than 1 cone; white cotton yarn (CC), about 10 yd (9 m) for scarf and face embroidery.

Rabbit	Cat	Teddy Bear
Height		
11	8¾	11"
28	22 cm	28 cm

Needles

Cat: U.S. size 5 (3.75 mm): straight.
Rabbit and Teddy Bear: U.S. size 7 (4.5 mm): straight.
Adjust needle size if necessary to obtain the correct gauge.

Notions

Tapestry needle; about 3½ oz (100 g) environmentally friendly stuffing; small crochet hook for attaching fringe to teddy bear's scarf (optional).

Gauge

Cat: 21 sts and 29 rows = 4" (10 cm) in St st.
Rabbit and Teddy Bear: 17 sts and 23 rows = 4" (10 cm) in St st.

Stitch Guide

Striped stockinette stitch:
Rows 1 and 3: (RS) Knit in MC.
Rows 2 and 4: Purl in MC.
Row 5: Knit in CC.
Row 6: Purl in CC.
Rep Rows 1-6 for pattern.

Cat

Body

With MC, CO 30 sts.
Work 50 rows in striped St st (see Stitch Guide).
Cut yarn, leaving a 20" (51-cm) tail. Thread tail through rem sts, pull tight to gather sts, and fasten off on inside. With yarn threaded on a tapestry needle, sew side edges together, leaving CO edge open.

Arms

With MC, CO 16 sts.
Work 18 rows in striped St st.
Cut yarn, leaving a 12" (30.5-cm) tail. Thread tail through rem sts, pull tight to gather sts, and fasten off on inside. With yarn threaded on a tapestry needle, sew side edges together, leaving CO edge open.

Legs

With MC, CO 18 sts.
Work 28 rows in striped St st.
Cut yarn, leaving a 14" (35.5-cm) tail. Thread tail through rem sts, pull tight to gather sts, and fasten off on inside. With yarn threaded on a tapestry needle, sew side edges together, leaving CO edge open.

Tail

With CC, CO 14 sts.
Working in St st, *work 4 rows CC, then 2 rows MC; rep from * 3 more times, then work 4 more rows CC.
Cut yarn, leaving a 14" (35.5-cm) tail. Thread tail through rem sts, pull tight to gather sts, and fasten off on inside. With yarn threaded on a tapestry needle, sew side edges together, leaving CO edge open.

Rabbit

Body, Arms, and Legs

Work as for cat body, arms, and legs, working in MC throughout.

Ears

With CC, CO 6 sts.
Work 36 rows in garter st.
Row 37: (dec row) K1, k2tog tbl, k2tog, k1—4 sts rem.
Row 38: Knit.
Row 39: (dec row) K2tog tbl, k2tog—2 sts rem.
Row 40: Knit.
Row 41: (dec row) K2tog—1 st rem.
Fasten off last st.

Teddy Bear

Body, Arms, and Legs

Work as for cat body, arms, and legs, working in MC throughout.

Scarf

With CC, CO 4 sts.
Work 100 rows in garter st.
BO all sts.

Finishing

Weave in loose ends. Using an environmentally friendly stuffing, stuff the body. Hold the body so that the seam lies at the back. Sew the CO end together into a flat seam from right to left, with the back seam at center back.

Cut a 20" (51-cm) length of yarn. Shape the head by wrapping the length of yarn several times around the stuffed body about one-third down from the CO edge. Tighten the yarn and secure.

Stuff the arms and legs and sew the CO end together as for body.

Sew the CO ends of legs on each side of the body about 1" (2.5 cm) up from base. Sew the CO ends of arms on each side of the body about 1" (2.5 cm) down from neck.

Cat

Stuff the tail and sew the CO end together as for body. Sew the CO end of tail on the back of the body about 1½" (3.8 cm) up from base on seam.

Cat and Teddy Bear

With MC threaded on a tapestry needle, sew diagonally across the top of the head to define the ears, then complete face embroidery using CC as shown in illustration. (See Glossary, page 120, for embroidery instructions.)

Teddy Bear

Cut 8 pieces of CC, each 3" (7.5 cm) long, for fringe. Attach 4 pieces of fringe to each end of scarf by folding fringe in half, pulling fold through end of scarf to form a loop, then pulling ends of fringe through this loop and tightening. (A crochet hook can be helpful for this.) Secure scarf tightly around teddy bear's neck.

Rabbit

Sew ears to top of head. With CC, make a 2" (5-cm) pom-pom (see Glossary, page 121) for tail and sew to body about 1½" (3.8 cm) up from base on seam at back.

With small amount of contrasting yarn threaded on a tapestry needle, embroider face as shown in illustration. (See Glossary, page 120, for embroidery instructions.)

Blanket and Hat

This easy-to-knit blanket and hat combination makes a great gift for a new baby. Both are useful and practical and, knitted in soft organic yarns, as delicate as the newborn wrapped within.

Yarn
Worsted weight (CYCA Medium #4): about 45 yd (41 m) for hat and 305 yd (279 m) for blanket.
Shown here: Blue Sky Alpacas Organic Cotton (100% organic cotton; 150 yd [137 m]/100 g): #83 sage, hat, less than 1 ball; blanket, 3 balls; both, 3 balls.
Needles
U.S. sizes 7 and 8 (4.5 and 5 mm): straight. Adjust needle size if necessary to obtain the correct gauge.
Notions
Tapestry needle.
Gauge
16 sts and 22 rows = 4" (10 cm) in St st on larger needles.

Hat

With smaller needles, CO 57 sts.
Beg with a knit row, work 4 rows in St st.
Change to larger needles.
Work 4 rows in garter st.
Work 6 rows in St st.
Work 4 rows in garter st.

Hat to fit newborn	
Finished circumference	
14¼"	36 cm
Blanket, Finished width	
18"	45.5 cm
Blanket, Finished length	
24"	61 cm

Shape crown:

Row 1: (RS; dec row) *K5, k2tog; rep from * to last st, k1—49 sts rem.

Rows 2–4: Beg with a purl row, work 3 rows in St st.

Row 5: *K4, k2tog; rep from * to last st, k1—41 sts rem.

Row 6: Purl.

Row 7: *K3, k2tog; rep from * to last st, k1—33 sts rem.

Row 8: Knit.

Row 9: *K2, k2tog; rep from * to last st, k1—25 sts rem.

Row 10: Knit.

Row 11: *K1, k2tog; rep from * to last st, k1—17 sts rem.

Row 12: Purl.

Row 13: *K2tog; rep from * to last st, k1—9 sts rem.

Cut yarn, leaving a 12" (30.5-cm) tail. Thread tail through rem sts, pull tight to gather sts, and fasten off on inside. Sew hat seam. Weave in loose ends. Block if desired.

Blanket

With smaller needles, CO 73 sts.

Work 8 rows in garter st.

Change to larger needles.

*Rows 1–6: Work in garter st.

Row 7: (RS) Knit.

Row 8: K8, p57, k8.

Rows 9–20: Rep Rows 7 and 8 six more times.

Rep from * 5 more times.

Work 6 rows in garter st.

Change to smaller needles.

Work 7 more rows in garter st, ending with a RS row. With WS facing, BO all sts knitwise. Weave in loose ends. Block if desired.

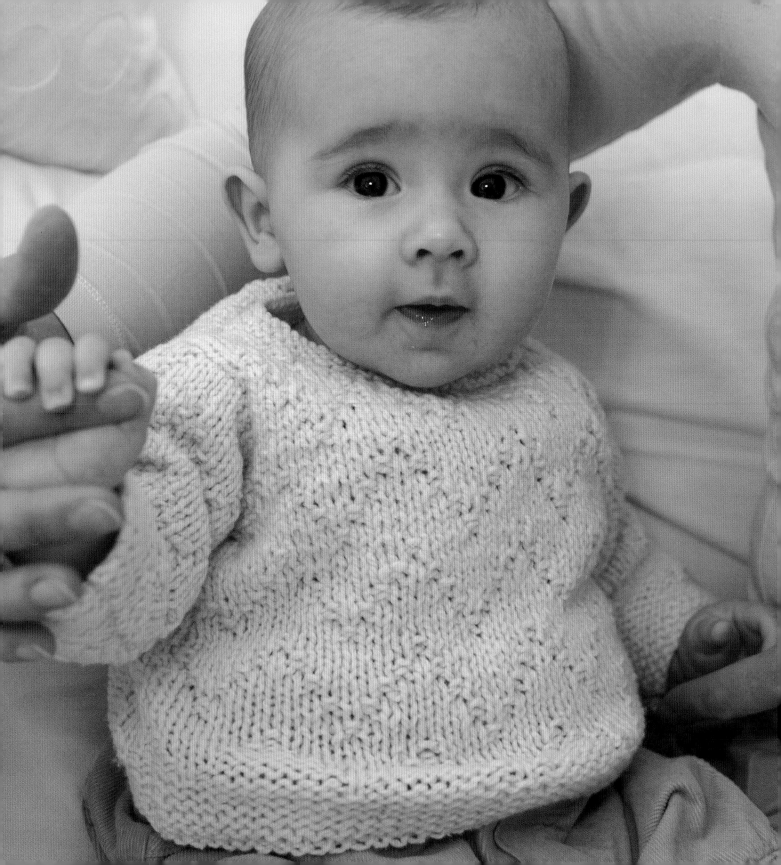

Fred Textured Sweater

A simple textured chevron stitch makes this lovely sweater a great baby garment—the simplicity of the stitch pattern ensures it will be a favorite to knit and to wear.

To fit ages			
newborn	up to 3 mos.	up to 6 mos.	up to 12 mos.
To fit chest circumference			
14	15½	17½	19"
40.5	45.5	51	56 cm
Finished chest circumference			
17	18½	20½	22"
43	47	52	56 cm
Width at underarm			
8½	9¼	10¼	11"
21.5	23.5	26	28 cm
Armhole depth			
4	4½	4¾	5"
10	11.5	12	12.5 cm
Neck width			
4¼	4½	5	5¼"
11	11.5	12.5	13.5 cm
Finished length			
9½	10	11	11¾"
24	25.5	28	30 cm
Sleeve length			
6¾	7½	8¾	10½"
17	19	22	26.5 cm

Shown here: Green Mountain Spinnery Cotton Comfort (20% organic cotton, 80% fine wool; 180 yd [165 m]/2 oz): #6-UW unbleached white, 2 (2, 3, 3) skeins. Sweater shown measures 17" (43 cm).

Needles
U.S. sizes 5 and 6 (3.75 and 4 mm): straight. Adjust needle size if necessary to obtain the correct gauge.

Notions
Stitch holders; tapestry needle; three ½" (1.3-cm) buttons, shown here in pearl.

Yarn
DK weight (CYCA Light #3): about 265 (300, 365, 435) yd (242 [274, 334, 398] m).

Gauge

22 sts and 30 rows = 4" (10 cm) in St st on larger needles.

Back

With smaller needles, CO 47 (51, 57, 61) sts.
Work in garter st for 10 rows.
Change to larger needles and, beg and end as indicated for your size, work Rows 1–8 of Chevron chart, then rep Rows 9–18 until piece measures 5½ (5½, 6¼, 6¾)" (14 [14, 16, 17] cm) from CO, ending with a WS row.

Shape armholes

BO 5 sts at beg of next 2 rows—37 (41, 47, 51) sts rem.
Work even until armholes measure 4 (4½, 4¾, 5)" (10 [11.5, 12, 12.5] cm), ending with a RS row.
Place sts on a holder.

Front

Work as for back until armholes measure 2¾ (3¼, 3½, 3¾)" (7 [8.5, 9, 9.5] cm), ending with a WS row.

Shape front neck

(RS) Work 11 (12, 14, 15) left front sts in patt; turn.
Place rem 26 (29, 33, 36) sts on a holder.
Work each side of neck separately.
Dec 1 st at neck edge every row 4 times—7 (8, 10, 11) sts rem.
Work even for 5 rows. Place sts on a holder.
Place center 15 (17, 19, 21) sts on a holder for neck.
With RS facing, rejoin yarn to 11 (12, 14, 15) right front sts. Work in patt to end of row.
Dec 1 st at neck edge every row 4 times—7 (8, 10, 11) sts rem. Work even for 5 rows. Place sts on a holder.

Sleeves

With smaller needles, CO 31 (31, 33, 35) sts.
Work in garter st for 10 rows.
(You will be increasing and following chart at the same time—read to the end of the sleeve directions before proceeding.)
Change to larger needles and beg and end as indicated for your size, work Rows 1–8 of Chevron chart, then rep Rows 9–18 of chart 3 (4, 4, 4) times,

☐	k on RS, p on WS
·	p on RS, k on WS
☐	pattern repeat

Chevron

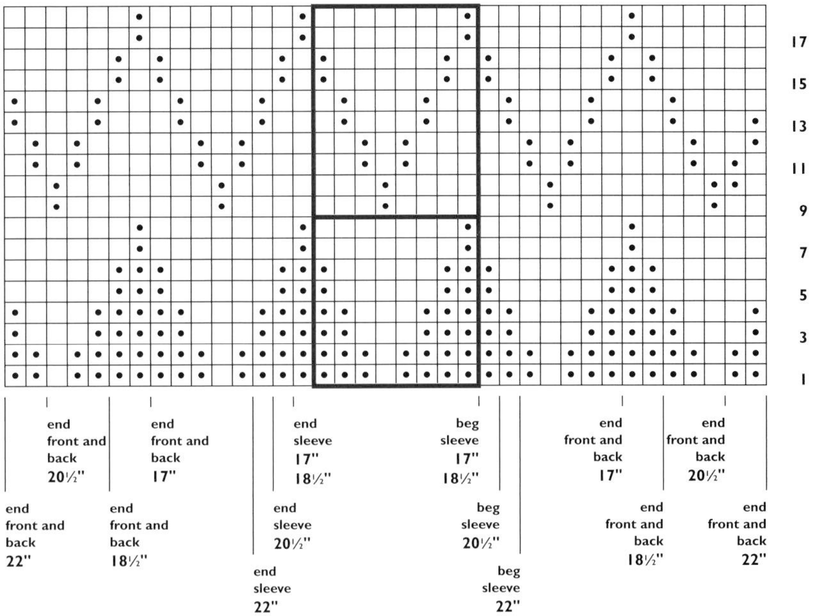

(knitting chart with rows numbered 1, 3, 5, 7, 9, 11, 13, 15, 17)

Bottom labels:
end front and back 20½"
end front and back 17"
end sleeve 17"
beg sleeve 17"
end front and back 17"
end front and back 20½"

end front and back 22"
end front and back 18½"
end sleeve 20½"
beg sleeve 20½"
end front and back 18½"
end front and back 22"

end sleeve 22"
beg sleeve 22"

and *at the same time* (beg with Row 1 of chart) inc 1 st at each end of needle every 6th row 5 (7, 7, 7) times, working inc sts into patt—41 (45, 47, 49) sts after all inc rows have been worked.

Work even in patt until piece measures 6¾ (7½, 8¾, 10½)" (17 [19, 22, 26.5] cm) from CO, ending with a WS row. BO all sts.

Finishing
Block pieces to measurements.

Place 7 (8, 10, 11) held right shoulder sts on smaller needles. With WS of front and back held tog and a larger needle, use the three-needle method (see Glossary, page 119) to join front to back at right shoulder.

Neck edging
With smaller needles, RS facing, and beg at left front shoulder, pick up and knit 10 sts along left front neck, k15 (17, 19, 21) held front neck sts, pick up and knit 10 sts along right front neck, and k23 (25, 27, 29) held back neck sts—58 (62, 66, 70) sts total. Leave rem 7 (8, 10, 11) back sts on holder for left back shoulder.

Work 4 rows in garter st, ending with a RS row. With WS facing, BO all sts knitwise.

Left back shoulder edging
With smaller needles and RS facing, pick up and knit 3 sts from back neck edging, k7 (8, 10, 11) held left back shoulder sts—10 (11, 13, 14) sts total. Beg with a WS row, work 2 rows in St st. With WS facing, BO all sts knitwise.

Left front shoulder edging
With smaller needles and RS facing, k7 (8, 10, 11) held left front shoulder sts, pick up and knit 3 sts from front neck edging—10 (11, 13, 14) sts total.

Next row: (WS; buttonhole row) P1 (1, 2, 2), [p2tog, yo, p1] 3 times, p0 (1, 2, 3).

Next row: Knit.

With WS facing, BO all sts knitwise.

With yarn threaded on a tapestry needle, sew sleeves into armholes. Sew side and sleeve seams. Weave in loose ends. Block again if desired. Sew on buttons opposite buttonholes.

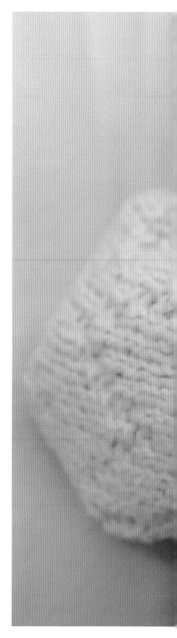

Jo Jo Basic Crew Sweater

This very simple sweater is transformed with beautiful lazy daisy embroidery around the eyelets on the girl's version and groovy stripes on the boy's. Who says a basic pattern has to look basic? Use the ideas shown here to customize your own version with embroidery or stripes.

To fit ages			
newborn	up to 3 mos.	up to 6 mos.	up to 12 mos.
To fit underarm circumference			
14	15½	17½	19"
35.5	39.5	44.5	48.5 cm
Finished underarm circumference			
17	18½	20½	22"
43	47	52	56 cm
Width at lower edge			
8½	9¼	10¼	11"
21.5	23.5	26	28 cm
Armhole depth			
4	4½	4¾	5"
10	11.5	12	12.5 cm
Neck width			
4¼	4½	5	5¼"
11	11.5	12.5	13.5 cm
Finished length			
9½	10	11	11¾"
24	25.5	28	30 cm
Sleeve length			
6¾	7½	8¾	10½"
17	19	22	26.5 cm

Yarn

DK weight (CYCA Light #3): about 190 (210, 260, 300) yd (174 [192, 238, 274] m) of MC and 85 (100, 120, 140) yd (78 [91, 110, 128] m) of CC for striped sweater, or 275 (310, 380, 440) yd (251 [283, 347, 402] m) and a small amount of CC for embroidered sweater.

Shown here: Green Mountain Spinnery Cotton Comfort (20% organic cotton, 80% fine wool; 180 yd [165 m]/2 oz): #6-B bluet (light blue, MC), 2 skeins (all sizes) and #6-D denim (dark blue, CC), 1 skein (all sizes) for striped sweater; #6-PL pink lilac, 2 (2, 3, 3) skeins and small amount of #6-MZ maize for embroidery. Striped sweater shown here measures 20½" (52 cm); embroidered sweater shown here measures 18½" (47 cm).

Needles

U.S. sizes 5 and 6 (3.75 and 4 mm): straight. Adjust needle size if necessary to obtain the correct gauge.

Notions

Stitch holders; tapestry needle; three ½" (1.3-cm) buttons, shown here in pearl.

Gauge

22 sts and 30 rows = 4" (10 cm) in St st on larger needles.

Striped Sweater
Back

With MC and smaller needles, CO 47 (51, 57, 61) sts.

Row 1: (RS) K1 (3, 0, 2), [p3, k3] 7 (7, 9, 9) times, p3, k1 (3, 0, 2).

Row 2: P1 (3, 0, 2), [k3, p3] 7 (7, 9, 9) times, k3, p1 (3, 0, 2).

Rep Rows 1–2 three more times.

Change to larger needles and CC and work in striped St st as foll:

Row 1: (RS) Knit in CC.

Row 2: Purl in CC.

Rows 3 and 5: Knit in MC.

Rows 4 and 6: Purl in MC.

Rep Rows 1–6 until piece measures 5½ (5½, 6¼, 6¾)" (14 [14, 16, 17] cm) from CO, ending with a WS row.

Shape armholes

BO 5 sts at beg of next 2 rows—37 (41, 47, 51) sts rem.

Work even, maintaining stripe patt, until armholes measure 4 (4½, 4¾, 5)" (10 [11.5, 12, 12.5] cm), ending with a RS row. Place sts on a holder.

Front

Work as for back until armholes measure 2¾ (3¼, 3½, 3¾)" (7 [8.5, 9, 9.5] cm), ending with a WS row.

Shape front neck

K11(12, 14, 15) left front sts; turn. Place rem 26 (29, 33, 36) sts on a holder.

Work each side of neck separately.

Maintaining stripe patt, dec 1 st at neck edge every row 4 times—7 (8, 10, 11) sts rem.

Work even for 5 rows. Place sts on a holder.

Leave center 15 (17, 19, 21) sts on holder for front neck.

With RS facing, rejoin yarn to 11 (12, 14, 15) right front sts. Knit 1 row.

Dec 1 st at neck edge every row 4 times—7 (8, 10, 11) sts rem. Work even for 5 rows. Place sts on a holder.

Sleeves

With MC and smaller needles, CO 31 (31, 33, 35) sts.

Row 1: (RS) K2 (2, 3, 4), [p3, k3] 4 times, p3, k2 (2, 3, 4).

Row 2: P2 (2, 3, 4), [k3, p3] 4 times, k3, p2 (2, 3, 4).

Rep Rows 1–2 three more times.

Change to larger needles and work in striped St st
as foll:

Rows 1 and 3: Knit in MC.

Rows 2 and 4: Purl in MC.

Rows 5 and 7: Knit in CC.

Rows 6 and 8: Purl in CC.

Rep Rows 1–8 for patt, and *at the same time* inc
1 st at each end of needle on first St st row, then
every 6th row 4 (6, 6, 6) more times—41 (45, 47, 49)
sts after all inc rows have been worked.

Work even until piece measures 6³/₄ (7¹/₂, 8³/₄, 10¹/₂)" (17 [19, 22, 26.5] cm) from CO, ending with a WS row. BO all sts.

Finishing

Block pieces to measurements. Place 7 (8, 10, 11) held right shoulder sts on smaller needles. With yarn to match shoulder, a larger needle, and holding WS of front and back together, use the three-needle method (see Glossary, page 119) to join front to back at right shoulder.

Neck edging

With smaller needles, MC, RS facing, and beg at left front shoulder, pick up and knit 10 sts along left front neck, k15 (17, 19, 21) held front neck sts, pick up and knit 10 sts along right front neck, and k23 (25, 27, 29) held back neck sts—58 (62, 66, 70) sts total. Leave rem 7 (8, 10, 11) back sts on holder for left back shoulder.

Row 1: (WS) [K2, p2] 14 (15, 16, 17) times, k2.
Row 2: [P2, k2] 14 (15, 16, 17) times, p2.
Rep Rows 1–2 once more, then rep Row 1 once more. BO all sts in rib.

Left back shoulder edging

With smaller needles, RS facing, and yarn color needed to maintain stripe patt, pick up and knit 3 sts from back neck edging, k7 (8, 10, 11) held left back shoulder sts—10 (11, 13, 14) sts total.
Beg with a purl row, work 2 rows in St st. BO all sts knitwise.

Left front shoulder edging

With smaller needles, RS facing, and yarn color needed to maintain stripe patt, k7 (8, 10, 11) held left front shoulder sts, pick up and knit 3 sts along front neck edging—10 (11, 13, 14) sts total.
Next row: (WS; buttonhole row) P1 (1, 2, 2), [p2tog, yo, p1] 3 times, p0 (1, 2, 3).
Next row: Knit.
With WS facing, BO all sts knitwise.
With yarn to match top of sleeve threaded on a tapestry needle, sew sleeves into armholes. Sew side and sleeve seams. Weave in loose ends. Block again if desired.
Sew on buttons opposite buttonholes.

Embroidered Sweater
Back

CO and work ribbing as for striped sweater back. Change to larger needles and, beg with a knit row, work 4 rows in St st.
Next row: (RS; eyelet row, optional) K2 (4, 1, 3), [yo, k2tog, k4] 7 (7, 9, 9) times, yo, k2tog, k1 (3, 0, 2).
Cont as for striped sweater back, working in one color throughout.

Front

Work as for embroidered sweater back through eyelet row.
Cont as for striped sweater front, working in one color throughout.

Sleeves

With smaller needles, CO 31 (31, 33, 35) sts.

Row 1: K2 (2, 3, 4), [p3, k3] 4 times, p3, k2 (2, 3, 4).

Row 2: P2 (2, 3, 4), [k3, p3] 4 times, k3, p2 (2, 3, 4).

Rep Rows 1 and 2 three more times.

Change to larger needles and, beg with a knit row, work 4 rows in St st, and *at the same time* inc 1 st at each end of needle on the first St st row—33 (33, 35, 37) sts.

Next row: (RS; eyelet row, optional) K4 (4, 5, 6), [yo, k2tog, k4] 4 times, yo, k2tog, k3 (3, 4, 5).

Cont as for striped sweater sleeve, working next inc on next RS row, and working in one color throughout.

Finishing

Finish as for striped sweater, working in one color throughout.

Embroidery (optional)

With CC threaded on a tapestry needle, work lazy daisy embroidery (see Glossary, page 120) around eyelets.

Jasmine Lace Edge Cardigan

Named after the bump inside the Bump Sweater on page 14, this elegant girl's cardigan has a delightful lace border, which is knitted lengthwise and sewn on.

Yarn

DK weight (CYCA Light #3): about 245 (280, 345, 405) yd (224 [256, 315, 370] m).

Shown here: Green Mountain Spinnery Cotton Comfort (20% organic cotton, 80% fine wool; 180 yd [165 m]/2 oz): #6-MI mint on page 58 and #6-WG weathered green on page 54, 2 (2, 2, 3) skeins. Mint sweater shown measures 18½" (47 cm); weathered green sweater shown measures 20½" (52 cm).

To fit ages			
newborn	up to 3 mos.	up to 6 mos.	up to 12 mos.
To fit chest circumference			
14	15½	17½	19"
35.5	39.5	44.5	48.5 cm
Finished chest circumference			
17	18½	20½	22"
43	47	52	56 cm
Back width			
8½	9¼	10¼	11"
21.5	23.5	26	28 cm
Front width			
4¼	4½	5	5½"
11	11.5	12.5	14 cm
Length of edging (from lower edge to top of edging)			
3	3	3	3"
7.5	7.5	7.5	7.5 cm
Length to underarm (excluding edging)			
2½	2½	3¼	3¾"
6.5	6.5	8.5	9.5 cm
Armhole depth			
4	4½	4¾	5"
10	11.5	12	12.5 cm
Back neck width			
3½	3½	3¾	4¼"
9	9	9.5	11 cm
Finished length			
9½	10	11	11¾"
24	25.5	28	30 cm
Sleeve length			
6¾	7½	8¾	10¼"
17	19	22	26 cm

Needles

U.S. sizes 5 and 6 (3.75 and 4 mm): straight. Adjust needle size if necessary to obtain the correct gauge.

Notions

Stitch holders; tapestry needle; four ½" (1.3-cm) buttons, shown here in pearl.

Gauge

22 sts and 30 rows = 4" (10 cm) in St st on larger needles.

Back

With smaller needles, CO 47 (51, 57, 61) sts.
Work 2 rows in garter st. Change to larger needles and, beg with a knit row, work in St st until piece measures 2½ (2½, 3¼, 3¾)" (6.5 [6.5, 8.5, 9.5] cm) from CO, ending with a WS row.

Shape armholes

BO 5 sts at beg of next 2 rows—37 (41, 47, 51) sts rem.
Work even until armholes measure 4 (4½, 4¾, 5)" (10 [11.5, 12, 12.5] cm), ending with a RS row. Place sts on a holder.

Left Front

With smaller needles, CO 23 (25, 28, 30) sts.
Work 2 rows in garter st. Change to larger needles and, beg with a knit row, work in St st until piece measures 2½ (2½, 3¼, 3¾)" (6.5 [6.5, 8.5, 9.5] cm) from CO, ending with a WS row.

Shape armhole and front neck

Next row: (RS) BO 5 sts, knit to last 2 sts, k2tog—17 (19, 22, 24) sts rem.

Purl 1 row.
Next row: Knit to last 2 sts, k2tog—16 (18, 21, 23) sts rem.
Purl 1 row.
Rep the last 2 rows 4 (4, 4, 6) more times—12 (14, 17, 17) sts rem.
Work 3 rows even in St st.
Dec 1 st at neck edge every 4th row 3 (3, 4, 3) times—9 (11, 13, 14) sts rem.
Work even until armhole measures 4 (4½, 4¾, 5)" (10 [11.5, 12, 12.5] cm), ending with a RS row. Place sts on a holder.

Right Front

With smaller needles, CO 23 (25, 28, 30) sts.
Work in garter st for 2 rows.
Change to larger needles and, beg with a knit row, work in St st until piece measures 2½ (2½, 3¼, 3¾)" (6.5 [6.5, 8.5, 9.5] cm) from CO, ending with a WS row.

Shape armhole and front neck

Next row: (RS) Ssk (see Glossary, page 120), knit to end—22 (24, 27, 29) sts rem.
Next row: BO 5 sts, purl to end—17 (19, 22, 24) sts rem.
Next row: Ssk, knit to end—16 (18, 21, 23) sts rem.
Purl 1 row.
Rep the last 2 rows 4 (4, 4, 6) more times—12 (14, 17, 17) sts rem.
Work 3 rows even in St st.
Dec 1 st at neck edge every 4th row 3 (3, 4, 3)

times—9 (11, 13, 14) sts rem.
Work even until armhole measures 4 (4½, 4¾, 5)"
(10 [11.5, 12, 12.5] cm), ending with a RS row. Place
sts on a holder.

Sleeves

With smaller needles, CO 35 (35, 37, 39) sts.
Work 2 rows in garter st. Change to larger needles
and, beg with a knit row, work in St st, and *at the
same time* inc 1 st at each end of needle on the 5
(5, 7, 7)th row once, then every 4 (4, 6, 6)th row 2
(4, 4, 4) times—41 (45, 47, 49) sts after all inc rows
have been worked.
Work even until piece measures 3¾ (4½, 5¾, 7¼)"
(9.5 [11.5, 14.5, 18.5] cm) from CO, ending with a
WS row.
BO all sts.

Finishing

Block pieces to measurements. Place 9 (11, 13, 14)
held shoulder sts on needles and use the three-
needle method (see Glossary, page 119) to join left
and right fronts to back at shoulders. Leave rem 19
(19, 21, 23) sts on holder for back neck.

Lace edging

With smaller needles, CO 13 sts.
Row 1: (RS) Knit.
Row 2: K2, yo, k2tog, k3, k2tog, yo, k2tog, [yo, k1]
    twice—14 sts.
Row 3: (picot edge) CO 2 sts, BO 2 sts, knit to end—
    14 sts.

Row 4: K2, yo, k2tog, k2, [k2tog, yo] twice, k3, yo, k1—15 sts.

Row 5: Knit.

Row 6: K2, yo, k2tog, k1, [k2tog, yo] twice, k5, yo, k1—16 sts.

Row 7: CO 2 sts, BO 2 sts, knit to end—16 sts.

Row 8: K2, yo, k2tog, k3, [yo, k2tog] twice, k1, k2tog, yo, k2tog—15 sts.

Row 9: Knit.

Row 10: K2, yo, k2tog, k4, yo, k2tog, yo, k3tog, yo, k2tog—14 sts.

Row 11: CO 2 sts, BO 2 sts, knit to end—14 sts.

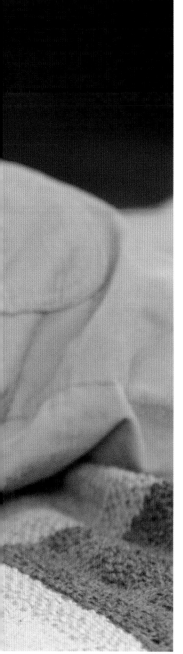

Row 12: K2, yo, k2tog, k5, yo, k3tog, yo, k2tog—13 sts.

Rep these 12 rows until edging measures 17 (18¼, 20¼, 22)" (43 [46.5, 51.5, 56] cm) from CO, or fits around bottom edge of cardigan. Place sts on a holder.

Work lace edging for sleeve cuffs as above, working until edging measures 6¼ (6¼, 6¾, 7)" (16 [16, 17, 18] cm) from CO. Sew sleeve lace edging to ends of sleeves, adjusting length if necessary by working more rows of edging if edging is too short or taking out rows if edging is too long. BO all sts. With yarn threaded on a tapestry needle, sew sleeves into armholes. Sew side and sleeve seams.

Sew bottom lace edging into place, adjusting length if necessary (as for sleeve edging). BO all sts.

Front edgings

With smaller needles, RS facing, and beg at right front lower edge, pick up and knit 13 sts along lace edging, 14 (14, 16, 18) sts along right front to start of front neck shaping, 22 (24, 26, 28) sts along right front neck to shoulder, k19 (19, 21, 23) held back neck sts, pick up and knit 22 (24, 26, 28) sts along left front neck, 14 (14, 16, 18) sts along left front to lace edging, and 13 sts from lace edging— 117 (121, 131, 141) sts total.

Next row: (WS) Knit.

Next row: (RS; buttonhole row) K1, [k2tog, yo, k6 (6, 7, 7)] 3 times, yo, k2tog, knit to end.

Work 2 rows in garter st.

With WS facing, work picot BO as foll:

BO 3 sts, *slip st from right needle to left needle, CO 2 sts, BO 5 sts; rep from * to end.

Weave in loose ends. Block again if desired. Sew on buttons opposite buttonholes.

Harvey Kimono

The kimono is a great design for a baby garment—it is very practical and looks smart. I have added a pretty picot edge to the girl's version.

To fit ages			
newborn	up to 3 mos.	up to 6 mos.	up to 12 mos.
To fit chest circumference			
14	15½	17½	19"
35.5	39.5	44.5	48.5 cm
Finished chest circumference			
17	18½	20½	22"
43	47	52	56 cm
Back width at lower edge/underarm			
8½	9¼	10¼	11"
21.5	23.5	26	28 cm
Armhole depth			
4	4½	4¾	5"
10	11.5	12	12.5 cm
Back neck width			
3½	3¼	4½	5"
9	9.5	11.5	12.5 cm
Front width at lower edge			
8½	9¼	10¼	11"
21.5	23.5	26	28 cm
Finished length (including edging)			
7½	8	9	9¾"
19	20.5	23	25 cm
Sleeve length (including edging)			
6¾	7½	8¾	10¼"
17	19	22	26 cm

Yarn

DK weight (CYCA Light #3): 280 (325, 395, 470) yd (256 [297, 361, 430] m).

Shown here: Green Mountain Spinnery Cotton Comfort (20% organic cotton, 80% fine wool; 180 yd [165 m]/2 oz): for girl's kimono #6-MZ maize, for boy's kimono #6-B bluet, 2 (2, 3, 3) skeins (either style). Sweaters shown measure 18½" (47 cm).

Needles

U.S. sizes 5 and 6 (3.75 and 4 mm): straight. Adjust needle size if necessary to obtain the correct gauge.

Notions

Stitch holders; tapestry needle; four ¾" (2-cm) buttons.

Gauge

22 sts and 30 rows = 4" (10 cm) in St st on larger needles.

Stitch Guide

Picot edge: Using the cable method (see Glossary, page 119), *CO 5 sts, BO 2 sts, slip st on right needle to left needle; rep from *—3 sts CO for each rep.

Girl's Kimono
Back

With smaller needles, work picot edge (see Stitch Guide) until there are 45 (51, 57, 60) sts on needle, then CO 2 (0, 0, 1) more st(s)—47 (51, 57, 61) sts. Work 8 rows in garter st. Change to larger needles and, beg with a RS row, work in St st until piece measures 3¹⁄₂ (3¹⁄₂, 4¹⁄₄, 4³⁄₄)" (9 [9, 11, 12] cm) from CO, ending with WS row.

Shape armholes

BO 5 sts at beg of next 2 rows—37 (41, 47, 51) sts rem. Work even until armholes measure 4 (4¹⁄₂, 4³⁄₄, 5)" (10 [11.5, 12, 12.5] cm), ending with a WS row. Place sts on a holder.

Left Front

With smaller needles, work picot edge until there are 45 (51, 57, 60) sts on needle, then CO 2 (0, 0, 1) more st(s)—47 (51, 57, 61) sts.

Work 5 rows in garter st.

Next row: (WS; buttonhole row) K2, k2tog, yo, knit to end.

Work 2 more rows in garter st.

Change to larger needles and, beg with a knit row, work in St st until piece measures 2 (2, 2, 2¹⁄₄)" (5 [5, 5, 5.5] cm) from CO, ending with a RS row.

Shape front edge

BO 5 (7, 7, 9) sts at beg of next row, then BO 5 sts at beg of foll WS row 2 (2, 3, 3) times—32 (34, 35, 37) sts rem.

BO 3 sts at beg of next WS row 1 (1, 3, 3) time(s)—29 (31, 26, 28) sts rem.

Dec 1 st at neck edge every row 0 (0, 3, 3) times—29 (31, 23, 25) sts rem.

Shape armhole and neck

BO 5 sts at beg of next RS row (armhole edge)—24 (26, 18, 20) sts rem.

BO 3 (3, 0, 0) sts at beg of next WS row 2 (2, 0, 0) times—18 (20, 18, 20) sts rem.

Dec 1 st at neck edge every row 3 (3, 0, 0) times, then every other row 6 (7, 4, 4) times, then every 4th row 0 (0, 3, 4) times—9 (10, 11, 12) sts rem. Work even until armhole measures 4 (4¹⁄₂, 4³⁄₄, 5)" (10 [11.5, 12, 12.5] cm), ending with a WS row. Place sts on a holder.

Right Front

With smaller needles, work picot edge until there are 45 (51, 57, 60) sts on needle, then CO 2 (0, 0, 1) additional st(s)—47 (51, 57, 61) sts.

Work 4 rows in garter st.

Row 5: (RS; buttonhole row) K1, k2tog, yo, knit to end.

Work 3 rows in garter st.

Change to larger needles and, beg with a RS row, work in St st until piece measures 2 (2, 2, 2¼)" (5 [5, 5, 5.5] cm) from CO, ending with a WS row.

Shape front edge

BO 5 (7, 7, 9) sts at beg of next row, then BO 5 sts at beg of every foll RS row 2 (2, 3, 3) times—32 (34, 35, 37) sts rem.

BO 3 sts at beg of next RS row 1 (1, 3, 3) time(s)—29 (31, 26, 28) sts rem.

Dec 1 st at neck edge every row 0 (0, 3, 3) times—29 (31, 23, 25) sts rem.

Shape armhole and neck

BO 5 sts at beg of next WS row (armhole edge)—24 (26, 18, 20) sts rem.

BO 3 (3, 0, 0) sts at beg of next RS row 2 (2, 0, 0) times—18 (20, 18, 20) sts rem.

Dec 1 st at neck edge every row 3 (3, 0, 0) times, then every other row 6 (7, 4, 4) times, then every 4th row 0 (0, 3, 4) times—9 (10, 11, 12) sts rem. Work even until armhole measures 4 (4½, 4¾, 5)" (10 [11.5, 12, 12.5] cm), ending with a WS row. Place sts on a holder.

Sleeves

With smaller needles, work picot edge until there are 30 (30, 33, 33) sts on needle, then CO 1 (1, 0, 2) st(s)—31 (31, 33, 35) sts.

Work 8 rows in garter st.

Change to larger needles and, beg with a knit row, work in St st, inc 1 st each end of needle every 6th row 5 (7, 7, 7) times—41 (45, 47, 49) sts.

Work even until piece measures 6¾ (7½, 8¾, 10¼)" (17 [19, 22, 26] cm), ending with a WS row. BO all sts.

Boy's Kimono

Work as for girl's kimono, using cable CO and omitting picot edge throughout.

Finishing

Block pieces to measurements. Place 9 (10, 11, 12) held shoulder sts on smaller needles. With a larger needle and holding RS of fronts and back together, use the three-needle method (see Glossary, page 119) to join fronts to back at shoulders. Leave rem 19 (21, 25, 27) sts on holder for back neck.

Front edgings

With smaller needles, RS facing, and beg at lower edge of right front shaping, pick up and knit 44 (50, 56, 62) sts from beg of shaping to shoulder, k19 (21, 25, 27) held back neck sts, pick up and knit 44 (50, 56, 62) sts from shoulder to end of left front shaping—107 (121, 137, 151) sts total.

Work 3 rows in garter st.

Next row: (RS; buttonhole row) K1, k2tog, yo, knit to last 3 sts, yo, k2tog, k1.

Work 2 rows in garter st.

Girl's Kimono

With WS facing, work picot BO as foll:

BO 3 sts, *slip st on right needle to left needle, CO 2 sts, BO 5 sts; rep from * to end.

Boy's Kimono

With WS facing, BO all sts knitwise.

Girl's and boy's kimonos side edging

With smaller needles, RS facing, and beg at right front lower edge, pick up and knit 20 (20, 22, 24) sts along buttonhole edge. Knit 2 rows. With WS facing, BO all sts knitwise. Rep for left front. With yarn threaded on a tapestry needle, sew sleeves into armholes. Sew side and sleeve seams. Weave in loose ends. Block again if desired.

Sew on buttons opposite buttonholes, wrapping right front over left for girl's kimono and left front over right for boy's kimono.

Adorable Chenille Cardigan

Knitted in soft chenille, this cardigan is perfect to snuggle a precious bundle and envelop the baby in softness and comfort.

Yarn

Worsted weight (CYCA Medium #4): 180 (210, 255, 310) yd (165 [192, 233, 283] m) chenille.
Shown here: Vreseis Fox Fibre Chenille (100% Col-organic cotton; 1000 yd [914 m]/16 oz): girl's cardigan shown on page 70 in green; boy's cardigan shown on page 67 in brown, less than 1 cone (all sizes). Sweaters shown measure 21" (53.5 cm).

Needles

U.S. sizes 7 and 8 (4.5 and 5 mm): straight. Adjust needle size if necessary to obtain the correct gauge.

To fit ages			
up to 3 mos.	up to 6 mos.	up to 12 mos.	up to 18 mos.
To fit chest circumference			
16½	19	21	23"
42	48.5	53.5	58.5 cm
Finished chest circumference			
18½	21	23	25"
47	53.5	58.5	63.5 cm
Width at back lower edge			
9¼	10½	11½	12½"
23.5	26.5	29	31.5 cm
Armhole depth			
4	4½	4¾	5"
10	11.5	12	12.5 cm
Back neck width			
4	4½	5	5½"
10	11.5	12.5	14 cm
Front width at lower edge			
4½	5	5½	6¼"
11.5	12.5	14	16 cm
Finished length			
9½	10	11	11¾"
24	25.5	28	30 cm
Sleeve length			
6¾	7½	8¾	10¼"
17	19	22	26 cm

Notions

Stitch holders; tapestry needle; four ½" (1.3-cm) buttons.

Gauge

15 sts and 24 rows = 4" (10 cm) in St st with larger needles.

Stitch guide

Seed stitch: (odd number of sts)

Row 1: *K1, p1; rep from * to last st, k1.

Rep Row 1 for pattern.

Back

With smaller needles, CO 35 (39, 43, 47) sts. Work in seed st (see Stitch Guide) for 6 rows. Change to larger needles and, beg with a knit row, work in St st until piece measures 5½ (5½, 6¼, 6¾)" (14 [14, 16, 17] cm) from CO, ending with a WS row.

Shape armholes

BO 4 sts at beg of next 2 rows—27 (31, 35, 39) sts rem. Work even until armholes measure 4 (4½, 4¾, 5)" (10 [11.5, 12, 12.5] cm), ending with a RS row. Place sts on a holder.

Left Front

With smaller needles, CO 17 (19, 21, 23) sts. Work in seed st for 6 rows.

Change to larger needles and, beg with a knit row, work in St st until piece measures 5½ (5½, 6¼, 6¾)" (14 [14, 16, 17] cm) from CO, ending with a WS row.

Shape armhole

BO 4 sts at beg of next row—13 (15, 17, 19) sts rem. Work even until armhole measures 2¼ (2¾, 3, 3¼)" (5.5 [7, 7.5, 8.5] cm), ending with a RS row.

Shape front neck

BO 4 (5, 6, 7) sts at beg of next row—9 (10, 11, 12) sts rem. Dec 1 st at neck edge every row 3 times—6 (7, 8, 9) sts rem. Work even until armhole measures 4 (4½, 4¾, 5)" (10 [11.5, 12, 12.5] cm), ending with a WS row. Place sts on a holder.

Right front

Work as for left front to arm-hole shaping, ending with a RS row.

Shape armhole

BO 4 sts at beg of next row—13 (15, 17, 19) sts rem. Work even until armhole measures 2¼ (2¾, 3, 3¼)" (5.5 [7, 7.5, 8.5] cm), ending with a WS row.

[B head] Shape front neck: BO 4 (5, 6, 7) sts at beg of next row—9 (10, 11, 12) sts rem. Dec 1 st at neck edge every row 3 times—6 (7, 8, 9) sts rem. Work even until armhole measures 4 (4½, 4¾, 5)" (10 [11.5, 12, 12.5] cm), ending with a WS row. Place sts on a holder.

Sleeves

With smaller needles, CO 23 (23, 25, 27) sts.
Work in seed st for 6 rows.

Change to larger needles and, beg with a knit row, work in St st, and *at the same time* inc 1 st each end of needle every 6 (6, 6, 8)th row 4 (6, 6, 6) times—31 (35, 37, 39) sts.

Work even until piece measures 6¾ (7½, 8¾, 10¼)" (17 [19, 22, 26] cm) from CO, ending with a WS row. BO all sts.

Finishing

Block to measurements. Place 6 (7, 8, 9) held shoulder sts on smaller needles and, with WS of cardigan fronts and back held together and a larger needle,

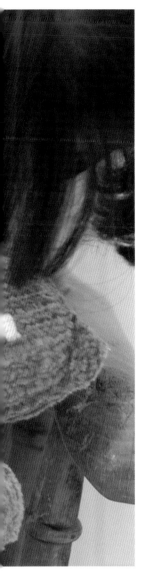

use the three-needle method (see Glossary, page 119) to join fronts to back at shoulders. Leave rem 15 (17, 19, 21) sts on holder for back neck.

Left front edging

With smaller needles, RS facing, and beg at neck edge, pick up and knit 29 (31, 33, 37) sts from neck edge to lower edge.

Girl's cardigan

Work in seed st for 4 rows. With WS facing, BO all sts knitwise.

Boy's cardigan

Row 1: Work in seed st.

Row 2: (RS; buttonhole row) [Work 7 (7, 8, 9) sts in seed st, yo, dec 1 st] 3 times, work in seed st to end. *Note:* Work dec as either k2tog or p2tog as needed to maintain seed st patt. Work in seed st for 2 rows. With WS facing, BO all sts knitwise.

Right front edging

With smaller needles, RS facing, and beg at lower edge, pick up and knit 29 (31, 33, 37) sts from lower edge to neck edge.

Boy's cardigan

Work in seed st for 4 rows. With WS facing, BO all sts knitwise.

Girl's cardigan

Row 1: Work in seed st.

Row 2: (RS; buttonhole row) K1, p1, [yo, dec 1 st, work 7 (8, 9, 10) sts in seed st] 2 times, yo, dec 1 st, work in seed st to end. *Note:* Work dec as either k2tog or p2tog as needed to maintain seed st patt.

Work in seed st for 2 rows. With WS facing, BO all sts knitwise.

Neck edging

With smaller needles and RS facing, pick up and knit 3 sts along right front band, 11 (12, 13, 14) sts along right front neck edge, k15 (17, 19, 21) held back neck sts, pick up and knit 11 (12, 13, 14) sts along left front neck edge, and 3 sts along left front band—43 (47, 51, 55) sts total. Work in seed st for 1 row.

Boy's cardigan

Row 2: (RS; buttonhole row) *K1, p1; rep from * to last 5 sts, k1, p2tog, yo, p1, k1.

Girl's cardigan

Row 2: (RS; buttonhole row) K1, p1, yo, p2tog, *k1, p1; rep from * to last st, k1.

Both cardigans

Work in seed st for 2 rows. With WS facing, BO all sts knitwise.

With yarn threaded on a tapestry needle, sew sleeves into armholes. Sew side and sleeve seams. Weave in loose ends. Block again if desired. Sew buttons onto band opposite buttonholes.

Kai Cable Sweater

This contemporary cable sweater is named after the very handsome young man in the photograph. Easy to knit and stylish, this sweater will become a great favorite with baby and mom.

Yarn
Worsted weight (CYCA Medium #4): about 200 (245, 305) yd (183 [224, 279] m).
Shown here: Blue Sky Alpacas Organic Cotton (100% cotton; 150 yd [137 m]/100 g): #82 nut, 2 (2, 3) balls. Sweater shown measures 22" (56 cm).

Needles
U.S. sizes 7 and 8 (4.5 and 5 mm): straight. Adjust needle size if necessary to obtain the correct gauge.

To fit ages		
up to 6 mos.	up to 12 mos.	up to 18 mos.
To fit chest circumference		
18	20	22"
45.5	51	56 cm
Finished chest circumference		
20	22	24"
51	56	61 cm
Width at underarm		
10	11	12"
25.5	28	30.5 cm
Armhole depth		
4½	4¾	5"
11.5	12	12.5 cm
Neck width		
4	4½	5"
10	11.5	12.5 cm
Finished length		
10	11	11¾"
25.5	28	30 cm
Sleeve length		
7½	8¾	10¼"
19	22	26 cm

Notions
Stitch holders; cable needle (cn); tapestry needle.

Gauge
16 sts and 22 rows = 4" (10 cm) in St st on larger needles.

Stitch guide

4/4RC: Sl 4 sts onto cn and hold in back, k4, k4 from cn.

Back

With smaller needles, CO 40 (44, 48) sts.

Row 1: (RS) K1, *k2, p2; rep from * to last 3 sts, k3.

Row 2: K1, *p2, k2; rep from * to last 3 sts, p2, k1.

Rep these 2 rows 4 more times. Change to larger needles and, beg with a knit row, work in St st until piece measures 5½ (6¼, 6¾)" (14 [16, 17] cm) from CO, ending with a WS row.

Shape armholes

BO 4 sts at beg of next 2 rows—32 (36, 40) sts rem. Work even until armholes measure 4½ (4¾, 5)" (11.5 [12, 12.5] cm), ending with a RS row. Place sts on a holder.

Front

With smaller needles, CO 40 (44, 48) sts.

Row 1: (RS) K1, p0 (2, 0), *k2, p2; rep from * to last 3 (1, 3) st(s), k3 (1, 3).

Row 2: K1 (3, 1), *p2, k2; rep from * to last 3 (1, 3) st(s), p2 (0, 2), k1.

Rows 3–9: Rep Rows 1 and 2 three more times, then work Row 1 once more.

Row 10: (WS; increase row) Work 19 (21, 23) sts in rib as established, M1 (see Glossary, page 122), k2, M1, work 19 (21, 23) sts in rib—42 (46, 50) sts.

Change to larger needles.

*Row 11: (RS) K15 (17, 19), p2, 4/4RC (see Stitch Guide), p2, k15 (17, 19).

Row 12: P15 (17, 19), k2, p8, k2, p15 (17, 19).

Row 13: K15 (17, 19), p2, k8, p2, k15 (17, 19).

Row 14: P15 (17, 19), k2, p8, k2, p15 (17, 19).

Rows 15–18: Rep Rows 13 and 14 two more times. Rep from * until piece measures 5½ (6¼, 6¾)" (14 [16, 17] cm) from CO, ending with a WS row.

Shape armholes

BO 4 sts at beg of next 2 rows—34 (38, 42) sts rem. Cont in patt as established until armholes measure 2¾ (3, 3¼)" (7 [7.5, 8.5] cm), ending with a WS row.

Shape front neck

K11 (13, 15) left front sts; place rem 23 (25, 27) sts on a holder. Working left side of neck only, dec 1 st at neck edge every row 3 (4, 5) times—8 (9, 10) sts rem. Work even until armhole measures 4½ (4¾, 5)" (11.5 [12, 12.5] cm), ending with a RS row. Place sts on a holder for left shoulder.

Leave center 12 sts on holder for front neck.

With RS facing, rejoin yarn to rem 11 (13, 15) right front sts. Knit 1 row.

Dec 1 st at neck edge every row 3 (4, 5) times—8 (9, 10) sts rem.

Work even until armhole measures 4½ (4¾, 5)" (11.5 [12, 12.5] cm), ending with a RS row.

Place sts on a holder for right shoulder.

Sleeves

With smaller needles, CO 24 (26, 28) sts.

Row 1: (RS) K1 (0, 1), *k2, p2; rep from * to last 3 (2, 3) sts, k3 (2, 3).

Row 2: K1 (0, 1), *p2, k2; rep from * to last 3 (2, 3) sts, p2, k1 (0, 1).

Rep Rows 1 and 2 four more times.

Change to larger needles and, beg with a RS row, work in St st, and *at the same time* inc 1 st each end of needle every 4 (4, 6)th row 6 times—36 (38, 40) sts.

Work even until piece measures 7½ (8¾, 10¼)" (19 [22, 26] cm) from CO, ending with a WS row. BO all sts.

Finishing

Block pieces to measurements. Place 8 (9, 10) held right shoulder sts on smaller needles and, with WS of front and back held together and a larger needle, use the three-needle method (see Glossary, page 119) to join front to back at shoulder. Leave rem 24 (27, 30) back sts on holder.

Neck edging

With smaller needles and RS facing, beg at left shoulder, pick up and knit 13 sts along left front neck, work 12 held front sts in patt, pick up and knit 12 sts along right front neck, k16 (18, 20) held back neck sts, pick up and knit 1 st at left shoulder—54 (56, 58) sts total. Leave rem 8 (9, 10) back sts on holder for left back shoulder.

Row 1: (WS) K1, p0 (2, 0), [k2, p2] 7 (7, 8) times, k2, p8, k2, [p2, k2] 3 times, k1.

Row 2: K1, [p2, k2] 3 times, p2, k8, p2, [k2, p2] 7 (7, 8) times, k1 (3, 1).

Rep Rows 1–2 once, then work Row 1 once more.

Next row: (RS; cable row) K1, [p2, k2] 3 times, p2, 4/4RC, p2, [k2, p2] 7 (7, 8) times, k1 (3, 1).

Next row: K1, p0 (2, 0), [k2, p2] 7 (7, 8) times, k2, p8, k2, [p2, k2] 3 times, k1.

Divide neck

Next row: (RS) K1, [p2, k2] 3 times, p2, k4, turn. Work each side of neck separately—19 sts.

Next row: P4, k2, [p2, k2] 3 times, k1.

Work 2 more rows in rib as established.

BO all sts in rib.

With RS facing, rejoin yarn to rem sts and work in patt to end—35 (37, 39) sts.

Work 3 rows even in rib as established.

BO all sts in rib.

Place 8 (9, 10) held left shoulder sts on smaller needles and, with WS of front and back held together and a larger needle, use the three-needle method to join front to back at shoulder. With yarn threaded on a tapestry needle, sew sleeves into armholes. Sew side and sleeve seams, leaving bottom rib open for side vents. Weave in loose ends. Block again if desired.

Geordie Stripe Yoke Jacket

This is a very simple design to knit. Experiment with your own color combinations—add in more colors if you are feeling adventurous.

To fit ages			
up to 3 mos.	up to 6 mos.	up to 12 mos.	up to 18 mos.
To fit chest circumference			
16	18	20	22"
40.5	45.5	51	56 cm
Finished chest circumference			
18½	20	22½	24"
47	51	57	61 cm
Width at underarm			
9¼	10	11¼	12"
23.5	25.5	28.5	30.5 cm
Armhole depth			
4	4½	4¾	5"
10	11.5	12	12.5 cm
Back neck width			
4	4½	4¾	5¼"
10	11.5	12	13.5 cm
Front width at lower edge			
4½	5	5½	6"
11.5	12.5	14	15 cm
Finished length			
9½	10	11	11¾"
24	25.5	28	30 cm
Sleeve length			
6¾	7½	8¾	10¼"
17	19	22	26 cm

Yarn

Worsted weight (CYCA Medium #4): about 190 (220, 270, 320) yd (174 [201, 247, 293] m) MC and 85 (100, 120, 140) yd (78 [91, 110, 128] m) CC.
Shown here: Vreseis Fox Fibre Cotton (100% Col-organic cotton; 840 yd [768 m]/1 lb), white (MC) and brown (CC), less than 1 cone each. Sweater shown measures 24" (61 cm).

Needles

U.S. sizes 5 and 6 (3.75 and 4 mm): straight. Adjust needle sizes if necessary to obtain the correct gauge.

Notions

Stitch holders; tapestry needle; five ⅝" (1.5-cm) buttons, shown here in mother-of-pearl.

Gauge

20 sts and 28 rows = 4" (10 cm) in St st on larger needles.

Stitch Guide

Striped stockinette stitch:

Row 1: (RS) Knit with CC.

Row 2: Purl with CC.

Rows 3 and 5: Knit with MC.

Rows 4 and 6: Purl with MC.

Rep Rows 1–6 for pattern.

Back

With CC and smaller needles, CO 46 (50, 56, 60) sts. Work in garter st for 6 rows.

Change to larger needles and MC and, beg with a RS row, work in St st until piece measures 5½ (5½, 6¼, 6¾)" (14 [14, 16, 17] cm) from CO, ending with a WS row.

Shape armholes

BO 4 sts at beg of next 2 rows—38 (42, 48, 52) sts rem.

Change to CC and work in striped St st (see Stitch Guide) until armholes measure 4 (4½, 4¾, 5)" (10 [11.5, 12, 12.5] cm), ending with a RS row. Place sts on holder.

Left Front

With CC and smaller needles, CO 23 (25, 28, 30) sts. Work in garter st for 6 rows. Change to larger needles and MC and, beg with a RS row, work in St st until piece measures 5½ (5½, 6¼, 6¾)" (14 [14, 16, 17] cm) from CO, ending with a WS row.

Shape armhole

(RS) BO 4 sts at beg of next row—19 (21, 24, 26) sts rem.

Purl 1 row. Change to CC and work in striped St st until armhole measures 2½ (3, 3¼, 3½)" (6.5 [7.5, 8.5, 9] cm), ending with a RS row.

Shape front neck

(WS) BO 6 (7, 8, 9) sts at beg of next row—13 (14, 16, 17) sts rem. Dec 1 st at neck edge every row 4 times—9 (10, 12, 13) sts rem.

Work even until armhole measures 4 (4½, 4¾, 5)" (10 [11.5, 12, 12.5] cm), ending with a RS row. Place sts on a holder.

Right Front

Work as for left front to armhole shaping, ending with a RS row.

Shape armhole

(WS) BO 4 sts at beg of next row—19 (21, 24, 26) sts rem.

Change to CC and work in striped St st until armhole measures 2½ (3, 3¼, 3½)" (6.5 [7.5, 8.5, 9] cm), ending with a WS row.

Shape front neck

(RS) BO 6 (7, 8, 9) sts at beg of next row—13 (14, 16, 17) sts rem. Dec 1 st at neck edge every row 4 times—9 (10, 12, 13) sts rem.

Work even until armhole measures 4 (4½, 4¾, 5)" (10 [11.5, 12, 12.5] cm), ending with a RS row. Place sts on a holder.

Sleeves

With CC and smaller needles, CO 30 (30, 32, 34) sts. Work in garter st for 6 rows.

Change to larger needles and MC and work in St st, and *at the same time* inc 1 st each end of needle every 4 (4, 6, 6)th row 6 (8, 8, 8) times—42 (46, 48, 50) sts.

Work even until piece measures 6¾ (7½, 8¾, 10¼)" (17 [19, 22, 26] cm) from CO, ending with a WS row. BO all sts.

Finishing

Block pieces to measurements. Place 9 (10, 12, 13) held shoulder sts on smaller needles and, with WS of pieces held together, a larger needle, and MC or CC as needed to maintain stripe patt, use the three-needle method (see Glossary, page 119) to join fronts to back at shoulders. Leave rem 20 (22, 24, 26) back neck sts on holder.

Right front edging

With CC, smaller needles, and RS facing, pick up and knit 40 (44, 48, 52) sts along right front edge. Work in garter st for 6 rows, ending with a RS row. With WS facing, BO all sts knitwise.

Left front edging

With CC, smaller needles, and RS facing, pick up and knit 40 (44, 48, 52) sts along left front edge. Work in garter st for 2 rows.

Buttonhole row: (WS) K1, [k2tog, yo, k7 (8, 9, 10)] 4 times, yo, k2tog, k1.

Work 3 rows in garter st. With WS facing, BO all sts knitwise.

Collar

With CC and smaller needles, CO 46 (50, 56, 60) sts. Work in garter st until piece measures 2 (2, 2½, 2½)" (5 [5, 6.5, 6.5] cm) from CO. BO all sts.

With MC threaded on a tapestry needle, sew sleeves into armholes. Sew side and sleeve seams. With CC, sew CO edge of collar in place, beg and ending at midpoint of each front band, and sewing to front necks and held back neck sts. Weave in loose ends. Block again if desired. Sew buttons onto right front band opposite buttonholes.

Milan Jacket

Appropriate for a boy or girl, this chunky jacket blends traditional and contemporary styling. The toggle buttons and button loops are reminders of a bygone age, but the simple textured stitch worked only on the sleeves makes this a fresh, modern design.

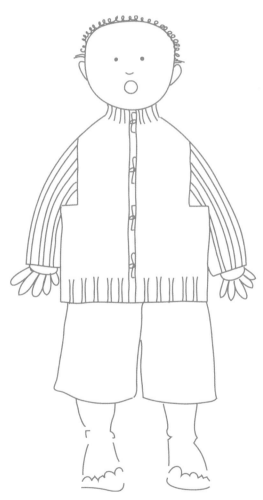

To fit ages		
up to 6 mos.	up to 12 mos.	up to 18 mos.
To fit chest circumference		
18	20	22"
45.5	51	56 cm
Finished chest circumference		
21	23½	25"
53.5	59.5	63.5 cm
Back underarm width		
10½	11¾	12½"
26.5	30	31.5 cm
Armhole depth		
4½	4¾	5"
11.5	12	12.5 cm
Back neck width		
4½	5	5½"
11.5	12.5	14 cm
Finished length		
11	12½	14"
28	31.5	35.5 cm
Sleeve length		
7½	8¾	10¼"
19	22	26 cm

Yarn

Worsted weight (CYCA Medium #4): about 335 (425, 505) yd (306 [389, 462] m).

Shown here: on page 84 in Vreseis Fox Fibre Cotton (100% Colorganic cotton; 840 yd [768 m]/1 lb): green, less than 1 cone; on page 87 in Garthenor

Organic Pure Wool Jacob (100% organic Jacob; 140 yd [128 m]/50 g), marl 3 (4, 4) balls. Sweaters shown measure 25" (63.5 cm).

Needles

U.S. sizes 5 and 6 (3.75 and 4 mm): straight. Adjust needle size if necessary to obtain the correct gauge.

Notions

Stitch holders; tapestry needle; size G/6 (4 mm) crochet hook; five 1" (2.5-cm) toggle buttons.

Gauge

20 sts and 28 rows = 4" (10 cm) in St st on larger needles.

Stitch Guide

Seed st rib: (multiple of 6 sts)

Row 1: (RS) *K1, p1, k4; rep from * across.

Row 2: *P3, k1, p1, k1; rep from * across.

Rep Rows 1 and 2 for pattern.

Back

With smaller needles, CO 53 (59, 63) sts.

Row 1: (RS) K1 (4, 0), work Row 1 of seed st rib (see Stitch Guide) to last 4 (1, 3) st(s), k1, p1 (0, 1), k2 (0, 1).

Row 2: P1 (0, 0), k1 (0, 1), p1 (0, 1), k1, work Row 2 of seed st rib to last 1 (4, 0) st(s), p1 (3, 0), k0 (1, 0).

Rep Rows 1 and 2 eight more times.

Change to larger needles and, beg with a RS row, work in St st until piece measures 6½ (7¾, 9)" (16.5 [19.5, 23] cm) from CO, ending with a WS row.

Shape armholes

(RS) BO 4 sts at beg of next 2 rows—45 (51, 55) sts rem.

Work even until armholes measure 4½ (4¾, 5)" (11.5 [12, 12.5] cm), ending with a RS row. Place sts on a holder.

Left Front

With smaller needles, CO 26 (29, 31) sts.

Row 1: (RS) K1 (4, 0), work Row 1 of seed st rib to last st, k1.

Row 2: K1, work Row 2 of seed st rib to last 1 (4, 0) st(s), p1 (3, 0), k0 (1, 0).

Rep Rows 1 and 2 eight more times. Change to larger needles and, beg with a RS row, work in St st until piece measures 6½ (7¾, 9)" (16.5 [19.5, 23] cm) from CO, ending with a WS row.

Shape armhole

BO 4 sts at beg of next row—22 (25, 27) sts rem. Work even until armhole measures 3 (3¼, 3½)" (7.5 [8.5, 9] cm), ending with a RS row.

Shape front neck

BO 7 (8, 9) sts at beg of next row—15 (17, 18) sts rem. Dec 1 st at neck edge every row 4 times—11 (13, 14) sts rem. Work even until armhole measures 4½ (4¾, 5)" (11.5 [12, 12.5] cm), ending with a RS row. Place sts on a holder.

Right Front

With smaller needles, CO 26 (29, 31) sts.

Row 1: (RS) K4, work Row 1 of seed st rib to last 4 (1, 3) st(s), k1, p1 (0, 1), k2 (0, 1).

Row 2: P1 (0, 0), k1 (0, 1), p1 (0, 1), k1, work Row 2 of seed st rib to last 4 sts, p3, k1.

Rep Rows 1 and 2 eight more times. Change to

larger needles and, beg with a RS row, work in St st until piece measures 6½ (7¾, 9)" (16.5 [19.5, 23] cm) from CO, ending with a RS row.

Shape armhole

BO 4 sts at beg of next row—22 (25, 27) sts rem. Work even until armhole measures 3 (3¼, 3½)" (7.5 [8.5, 9] cm), ending with a WS row.

Shape front neck

BO 7 (8, 9) sts at beg of next row—15 (17, 18) sts rem. Dec 1 st at neck edge every row 4 times—11 (13, 14) sts rem. Work even until armhole measures 4½ (4¾, 5)" (11.5 [12, 12.5] cm), ending with a RS row. Place sts on a holder.

Sleeves

With smaller needles, CO 33 (35, 37) sts.

Row 1: (RS) P0 (0, 1), k3 (4, 4), work Row 1 of seed st rib to last 0 (1, 2) st(s), k0 (1, 1), p0 (0, 1).

Row 2: P0 (0, 1), k0 (1, 1), work Row 2 of seed st rib to last 3 (4, 5) sts, p3, k0 (1, 1), p0 (0, 1).

Rep Rows 1 and 2 four more times.

Change to larger needles and cont to rep Rows 1 and 2 for patt, and *at the same time* inc 1 st each end of needle every 4 (6, 6)th row 7 times, working inc sts into patt—47 (49, 51) sts, after all inc rows have been worked.

Work even until piece measures 7½ (8¾, 10¼)" (19 [22, 26] cm) from CO, ending with a WS row. BO all sts.

Finishing

Block pieces to measurements. Place 11 (13, 14) held shoulder sts on smaller needles. With WS of fronts and back held together and a larger needle, use the three-needle method (see Glossary, page 119) to join fronts to back at shoulders. Leave rem 23 (25, 27) back sts on holder for back neck.

Neck edging

With smaller needles. RS facing, and beg at right front edge, pick up and knit 12 (13, 14) sts from right front neck, k23 (25, 27) held back neck sts, and pick up and knit 12 (13, 14) sts from left front neck—47 (51, 55) sts total.

Row 1: (WS) P0 (0, 1), k1 (0, 1), work Row 2 (WS row) of seed st rib to last 4 (3, 5) sts, p3, k1 (0, 1), p0 (0, 1).

Row 2: P0 (0, 1), k1 (3, 4), work Row 1 of seed st rib to last 1 (0, 2) st(s), k1 (0, 1), p0 (0, 1).

Rep Rows 1 and 2 until edging measures 2" (5 cm), ending with a RS row. With WS facing, BO all sts knitwise.

Left front edging

With smaller needles, RS facing, and beg at top of neck edging, pick up and knit 60 (66, 74) sts along left front edge. Work 2 rows in garter st. With WS facing, BO all sts knitwise.

Right front edging

With smaller needles, RS facing, and beg at lower edge, pick up and knit 60 (66, 74) sts along right front edge to top of neck edging. Work 2 rows in garter st. With WS facing, BO all sts knitwise.

With yarn threaded on a tapestry needle, sew sleeves into armholes.

Sew side and sleeve seams.

Button loop (make 5)

With crochet hook and leaving a tail, ch 8. Fasten off, leaving another tail. Attach button loops to front edge, attaching to right front for girl's jacket and to left front for boy's jacket, placing top loop at base of neck edging, bottom loop about 1½" (3.8 cm) from lower edge, and rem 3 loops evenly spaced between. Weave in loose ends. Block again if desired.

Sew buttons onto band opposite button loops.

Amelie Dress

I love to dress little girls in knitted slipover dresses—they are so simple and versatile! This design is worked in two colors, and the flowers are knitted separately and sewn on. You can change the look easily by using only one shade for the dress and lots of colors for the flowers, grouping them in bunches, and adding stems with embroidery. Let your imagination go!

To fit ages		
up to 3 mos.	up to 6 mos.	up to 12 mos.
To fit chest circumference		
16	18	20"
40.5	45.5	51 cm
Finished chest circumference		
18	20	21½"
45.5	51	54.5 cm
Width at underarm		
9	10	10¾"
23	25.5	27.5 cm
Armhole depth		
4½	4¾	5"
11.5	12	12.5 cm
Neck width		
3½	4¼	4½"
9	11	11.5 cm
Finished length		
14	15	17"
35.5	38	43 cm

Yarn

DK weight (CYCA Light #3): about 240 (285, 345) yd (219 [261, 315] m) of MC and 60 (70, 80) yd (55 [64, 73] m) of CC.

Shown here: Green Mountain Spinnery Cotton Comfort (20% organic cotton, 80% fine wool; 180 yd [165 m]/2 oz): #6-V violet (MC), 2 skeins (all sizes) and #6-PL pink lilac (CC), 1 skein (all sizes). Dress shown measures 21½" (54.5 cm).

Needles

U.S. sizes 5 and 6 (3.75 and 4 mm): straight. Adjust needle size if necessary to obtain the correct gauge.

Notions

Stitch holders; tapestry needle; two (three, three) ½" (1.3-cm) buttons.

Gauge

22 sts and 30 rows = 4" (10 cm) in St st on larger needles.

Notes

The flowers are knitted separately and attached. Sixteen are made in MC and eight are made in CC.

Back

With MC and smaller needles, CO 65 (71, 75) sts. Work in garter st for 8 rows. Change to CC and larger needles and, beg with a RS row, work 20 rows in St st. Change to MC and work 2 rows in St st.

Next row: (RS; dec row) K3, k2tog, knit to last 5 sts, k2tog through back loop (tbl), k3—2 sts dec'd. Work 3 (3, 5) rows even in St st. Rep the last 4 (4, 6) rows 7 more times—49 (55, 59) sts rem.

Work even in St st until piece measures 9½ (10¼, 12)" (24 [26, 30.5] cm) from CO, ending with a WS row.

Shape armholes

BO 4 sts at beg of next 2 rows—41 (47, 51) sts rem. Dec 1 st each end of needle every row 3 times—35 (41, 45) sts rem.

Work even until armholes measure 4½ (4¾, 5)" (11.5 [12, 12.5] cm), ending with a RS row. Place sts on a holder.

Front

Work as for back until armholes measure 3 (3¼, 3½)" (7.5 [8.5, 9] cm), ending with a WS row.

Shape front neck

K11 (12, 13) left front sts, turn. Place rem 24 (29, 32) sts on a holder.

Working left side of neck only, dec 1 st at neck edge every row 3 times—8 (9, 10) sts rem. Work even until armhole measures 4½ (4¾, 5)" (11.5 [12, 12.5] cm), ending with a RS row. Place sts on a holder.

Leave center 13 (17, 19) sts on holder for front neck.

With RS facing, rejoin MC to rem 11 (12, 13) right front sts and knit to end.

Dec 1 st at neck edge every row 3 times—8 (9, 10) sts rem.

Work even until armhole measures 4½ (4¾, 5)" (11.5 [12, 12.5] cm), ending with a RS row. Place sts on a holder.

Finishing

Block pieces to measurements.

Place held 8 (9, 10) right shoulder sts onto smaller needles. With MC, a larger needle, and WS of front and back held together, use the three-needle method (see Glossary, page 119) to join front to back at right shoulder. Leave rem 27 (32, 35) back sts on holder.

Neck edging

With MC, smaller needles, RS facing, and beg at left shoulder, pick up and knit 10 sts from left front neck, k13 (17, 19) held front neck sts, pick up and knit 10 sts along right front neck, and k19 (23, 25) held back neck sts—52 (60, 64) sts total. Leave rem 8 (9, 10) back sts on holder for left back shoulder. Work 2 rows in garter st. With WS facing, BO all sts knitwise.

Left back shoulder edging

With MC, smaller needles, and RS facing, pick up and knit 2 sts from back neck edging, then k8 (9, 10) held left back shoulder sts—10 (11, 12) sts total. Work 2 rows in St st. With WS facing, BO all sts knitwise.

Left front shoulder edging

With MC, smaller needles, and RS facing, k8 (9, 10) held left front shoulder sts, pick up and knit 2 sts from neck edging—10 (11, 12) sts total.

Next row: (WS; buttonhole row) P2 (1, 1), [p2tog, yo, p1] 2 (3, 3) times, p2 (1, 2).

Next row: Knit.

With WS facing, BO all sts knitwise. With MC threaded on a tapestry needle, sew shoulder edgings together at armhole edge, wrapping front shoulder edging over back shoulder edging.

Armhole edging

With MC, smaller needles, RS facing, and beg at front lower edge of left armhole, pick up and knit 22 (24, 26) sts from lower edge to shoulder and 22 (24, 26) sts from shoulder to back lower armhole edge—44 (48, 52) sts total.

Work 2 rows in garter st.

With WS facing, BO all sts knitwise. Rep for right armhole edge, beg at back lower edge of armhole. With MC threaded on a tapestry needle, sew side seams, leaving garter st edging at hem open for vent. Weave in loose ends. Block again if desired. Sew on buttons opposite buttonholes.

Flowers (make 16 in MC and 8 in CC)

With larger needles, CO 36 sts.

Row 1: *K1, BO 4 sts; rep from * to end—12 sts rem. Cut yarn, leaving a 12" (30.5-cm) tail. Thread through rem sts, pull tight to gather sts, and fasten off. Sew flowers onto dress as illustrated.

Oz Vest

This design is inspired by my little boy. Vests are practical for active babies, as they provide warmth around the body but do not restrict movement. After all, babies don't stay still for long, with all that crawling and exploring to do!

To fit ages			
newborn	up to 3 mos.	up to 6 mos.	up to 12 mos.
To fit chest circumference			
14½	16	18	20"
40.5	45.5	51	56 cm
Finished chest circumference			
16½	18	20	21½"
42	45.5	51	54.5 cm
Underarm width			
8¼	9	10	10¾"
21	23	25.5	27.5 cm
Armhole depth			
4	4½	4¾	5"
10	11.5	12	12.5 cm
Neck width			
3	3½	4¼	4½
7.5	9	11	11.5 cm
Finished length			
9½	10	11	11¾"
24	25.5	28	30 cm

Yarn
DK weight (CYCA Light #3): about 155 (185, 215, 250) yd (142 [169, 197, 229] m).
Shown here: Green Mountain Spinnery Cotton Comfort (20% organic cotton, 80% fine wool; 180 yd [165 m]/2 oz): #6-WG weathered green, 1 (2, 2, 2) skeins. Vest shown measures 20" (51 cm).
Needles
U.S. sizes 5 and 6 (3.75 and 4 mm): straight. Adjust needle size if necessary to obtain the correct gauge.
Notions
Stitch holders; tapestry needle; two (two, three, three) ½" (1.3-cm) buttons.
Gauge
22 sts and 30 rows = 4" (10 cm) in St st on larger needles.

Stitch Guide

Textured stripe pattern:

Row 1 and all odd-numbered rows: (RS) Knit.

Rows 2 and 4: Purl.

Rows 6 and 8: Knit.

Row 10: Purl.

Rep Rows 1–10 for pattern.

Back

With smaller needles, CO 45 (49, 55, 59) sts.
Work in garter st for 8 rows.

Change to larger needles and work in textured stripe patt (see Stitch Guide) until piece measures 5½ (5½, 6¼, 6¾)" (14 [14, 16, 17] cm) from CO, ending with a WS row.

Shape armholes

BO 4 sts at beg of next 2 rows—37 (41, 47, 51) sts rem.

Dec 1 st each end of needle every row 3 times—31 (35, 41, 45) sts rem.

Work even until armholes measure 4 (4½, 4¾, 5)" (10 [11.5, 12, 12.5] cm), ending with a RS row. Place sts on a holder.

Front

Work as for back until piece measures 5½ (5½, 6¼, 6¾)" (14 [14, 16, 17] cm) from CO, ending with a WS row.

Shape armholes and front neck

BO 4 sts at beg of next row, then work in patt until there are 18 (20, 23, 25) sts on right needle. Place rem 23 (25, 28, 30) sts on a holder for right front. Work each side of neck separately.

Dec 1 st at armhole edge every row 4 times, and *at the same time* dec 1 st at neck edge every other row 7 (8, 10, 11) times—7 (8, 9, 10) sts rem.

Work even until armhole measures 4 (4½, 4¾, 5)" (10 [11.5, 12, 12.5] cm), ending with a RS row. Place sts on a holder.

With RS facing, rejoin yarn to 23 (25, 28, 30) held right front sts, BO 1 st, knit to end of row—22 (24, 27, 29) sts rem.

Row 1: (WS) BO 4 sts, work in patt to end of row—18 (20, 23, 25) sts rem.

Dec 1 st at armhole edge every row 4 times, and *at the same time* dec 1 st at neck edge every other row 7 (8, 10, 11) times—7 (8, 9, 10) sts rem.

Work even until armhole measures 4 (4½, 4¾, 5)" (10 [11.5, 12, 12.5] cm), ending with a RS row. Place sts on a holder.

Finishing

Block pieces to measurements.

Place 7 (8, 9, 10) held right shoulder sts on smaller needles. With RS tog and a larger needle, use the three-needle method (see Glossary, page 119) to join front to back at right shoulder.

Neck edging

With smaller needles and RS facing, beg at left shoulder, pick up and knit 21 (23, 25, 27) sts along left front neck, 1 st at center front, 21 (23, 25, 27) sts along right front neck, and k17 (19, 23, 25) held

back neck sts—60 (66, 74, 80) sts total. Leave rem 7 (8, 9, 10) back sts on holder for left back shoulder. Work 2 rows in garter st.

With WS facing, BO all sts knitwise.

Left back shoulder edging

With smaller needles and RS facing, pick up and knit 2 sts from back neck edging, k7 (8, 9, 10) held left back shoulder sts—9 (10, 11, 12) sts total.

Work 2 rows in St st, ending with a RS row. With WS facing, BO all sts knitwise.

Left front shoulder edging

With smaller needles and RS facing, k7 (8, 9, 10) held left front shoulder sts, and pick up and knit 2 sts from neck edging—9 (10, 11, 12) sts total.

Next row: (WS; buttonhole row) P2 (2, 1, 1), [p2tog, yo, p1] 2 (2, 3, 3) times, p1 (2, 1, 2).

Next row: Knit.

With WS facing, BO all sts knitwise.

With yarn threaded on a tapestry needle, sew shoulder edgings together at armhole edge, wrapping front shoulder edging over back shoulder edging.

Armhole edging

With smaller needles, RS facing, and beg at front lower edge of left armhole, pick up and knit 22 (24, 26, 28) sts from lower edge to shoulder and 22 (24, 26, 28) sts from shoulder to back lower armhole edge—44 (48, 52, 56) sts total.

Work 2 rows in garter st.

With WS facing, BO all sts knitwise. Rep for right armhole, beg at back lower edge of armhole.

With yarn threaded on a tapestry needle, sew side seams, leaving garter st edging at hem open for vent. Block again if desired. Sew on buttons opposite buttonholes.

Queen of Hearts Nursing Sweater

This sweater's shape is inspired by the 1950s, but its purpose will never go out of date. With its cute heart motifs, this garment cleverly hides its ultimate purpose as a nursing sweater. Undo the buttons on either side for discreet mother-and-baby moments.

To fit bust circumference			
32–34	36–38	40–42	44–46"
81.5–86.5	91.5–96.5	101.5–106.5	112–117 cm
Finished bust circumference			
40½	43½	46½	49½"
103	110.5	118	125.5 cm
Underarm width			
20¼	21¾	23¼	24¾"
51.5	55	59	63 cm
Armhole depth			
8¼	8¼	9	9"
21	21	23	23 cm
Neck width			
8¾	8¾	8¾	8¾"
22	22	22	22 cm
Finished length			
22	23	24	25"
56	58.5	61	63.5 cm
Sleeve length to underarm/cap			
14	14	15	15"
35.5	35.5	38	38 cm

Yarn
Worsted weight (CYCA Medium #4): about 790 (855, 950, 1015) yd (722 [782, 869, 928] m).
Shown here: Blue Sky Alpacas Organic Cotton (100% organic cotton; 150 yd [137 m]/100 g): #81 sand, 6 (6, 7, 7) balls. Sweater shown measures 43½" (110.5 cm).

Needles
U.S. sizes 7 and 8 (4.5 and 5 mm): straight. Adjust needle size if necessary to obtain the correct gauge.

Notions

Stitch holders; markers (m); tapestry needle; fourteen (fourteen, sixteen, sixteen) ⁵⁄₈" (1.5-cm) buttons.

Gauge

16 sts and 22 rows = 4" (10 cm) in St st on larger needles.

Stitch Guide

Seed stitch: (odd number of sts)

Row 1: *K1, p1; rep from * to last st, k1.

Rep Row 1 for pattern.

Back

With smaller needles, CO 91 (97, 103, 109) sts. Work in seed st (see Stitch Guide) for 10 rows. Change to larger needles.

Row 11: (RS; dec row) K2tog, k26 (28, 30, 32), work 4 sts in seed st, k27 (29, 31, 33), work 4 sts in seed st, k26 (28, 30, 32), k2tog—89 (95, 101, 107) sts rem.

Row 12: P27 (29, 31, 33), work 4 sts in seed st, p27 (29, 31, 33), work 4 sts in seed st, p27 (29, 31, 33).

Rows 13–14: Work even in St st and seed st as established.

Row 15: (RS; pattern set-up row) [K5 (6, 7, 8), place marker (pm), work Row 1 of Heart chart (page 106), pm, k5 (6, 7, 8), work 4 sts in seed st] twice, k5 (6, 7, 8), pm, work Row 1 of Heart chart, pm, k5 (6, 7, 8).

Row 16: [Purl to m, work Row 2 of Heart chart, p5 (6, 7, 8), work 4 sts in seed st] twice, purl to m, work Row 2 of Heart chart, p5 (6, 7, 8).

Rows 17–20: Work in St st, seed st, and follow Heart chart as established.

Row 21: (RS; dec row) K2tog, knit to m, work Row 7 of Heart chart, k5 (6, 7, 8), work 4 sts in seed st, knit to m, work Row 7 of Heart chart, k5 (6, 7, 8), work 4 sts in seed st, knit to m, work Row 7 of Heart chart, k3 (4, 5, 6), k2tog—87 (93, 99, 105) sts rem.

Rows 22–30: Work even as established, following Heart chart.

Row 31: (RS; dec row) K2tog, knit to m, work Row 17 of Heart chart, k5 (6, 7, 8), work 4 sts in seed st, knit to m, work Row 17 of Heart chart, k5 (6, 7, 8), work 4 sts in seed st, knit to m, work Row 17 of Heart chart, k2 (3, 4, 5), k2tog—85 (91, 97, 103) sts rem.

Rows 32–40: Work even as established to end of Heart chart, removing markers on last row.

Row 41: (RS; dec row) K2tog, k23 (25, 27, 29), work 4 sts in seed st, k27 (29, 31, 33), work 4 sts in seed st, k23 (25, 27, 29), k2tog—83 (89, 95, 101) sts rem.

Rows 42–44: Work even in St st and seed st as established.

Rows 45–50: Work even in seed st.

Row 51: (RS; dec row) K2tog, k22 (24, 26, 28), work 4 sts in seed st, k27 (29, 31, 33), work 4 sts in seed st, k22 (24, 26, 28), k2tog—81 (87, 93, 99) sts rem.

Work even in St st and seed st until piece measures 13 (14, 14¼, 15¼)" (33 [35.5, 36, 38.5] cm) from CO, ending with a WS row.

Shape armhole

BO 4 sts at beg of next 2 rows, then BO 3 sts at beg of foll 2 rows—67 (73, 79, 85) sts rem.

Dec 1 st each end of needle every row 3 times, then dec 1 st each end of needle every other row 0 (1, 2, 3) time(s)—61 (65, 69, 73) sts rem.

Work even until armholes measure 5¾ (5¾, 6½, 6½)" (14.5 [14.5, 16.5, 16.5] cm), ending with a WS row.

Work 14 rows even in seed st.

Shape shoulders and back neck

BO 4 (5, 6, 6) sts at beg of next row, work in seed st until there are 15 (16, 17, 19) sts on right needle. Place rem 42 (44, 46, 48) sts on a holder for left back—15 (16, 17, 19) sts rem.

Work each side of neck separately.

Next row: (WS) BO 3 sts, work in seed st to end of row—12 (13, 14, 16) sts rem.

Next row: BO 4 (5, 6, 6) sts, work in seed st to end of row—8 (8, 8, 10) sts rem.

Next row: BO 3 sts, work in seed st to end of row—5 (5, 5, 7) sts rem.

BO rem 5 (5, 5, 7) sts.

Leave center 23 sts on holder for back neck. With RS facing, rejoin yarn to rem 19 (21, 23, 25) held sts and work in seed st to end of row.

Next row: (WS) BO 4 (5, 6, 6) sts at beg of next row—15 (16, 17, 19) sts rem.

Next row: BO 3 sts, work in seed st to end of row—12 (13, 14, 16) sts rem.

Next row: BO 4 (5, 6, 6) sts, work in seed st to end of row—8 (8, 8, 10) sts rem.

Next row: BO 3 sts, work in seed st to end of row—5 (5, 5, 7) sts rem.

BO rem 5 (5, 5, 7) sts.

Left Front Panel

With smaller needles, CO 32 (34, 36, 38) sts.

Work in seed st for 10 rows.

Change to larger needles.

Row 11: (RS; dec row) K2tog, k26 (28, 30, 32), work 4 sts in seed st—31 (33, 35, 37) sts rem.

Row 12: Work 4 sts in seed st, purl to end of row.

Row 13: Knit to last 4 sts, work 4 sts in seed st.

Row 14: Work 4 sts in seed st, purl to end of row.

Row 15: (RS; pattern set-up row) K5 (6, 7, 8), pm, work Row 1 of Heart chart, pm, k5 (6, 7, 8), work 4 sts in seed st.

Row 16: Work 4 sts in seed st, purl to m, work Row 2 of Heart chart, p5 (6, 7, 8).

Rows 17–20: Work in St st, seed st, and Heart chart as established.

Row 21: (RS; dec row) K2tog, knit to m, work Row 7 of Heart chart, k5 (6, 7, 8), work 4 sts in seed st—30 (32, 34, 36) sts rem.

Rows 22–30: Work even in patt, following Heart chart as established.

Row 31: (RS; dec row) K2tog, knit to m, work Row 17 of Heart chart, k5 (6, 7, 8), work 4 sts in seed st—29 (31, 33, 35) sts rem.

Rows 32–40: Work even as established to end of Heart chart, removing markers on last row.

Row 41: (RS; dec row) K2tog, knit to last 4 sts, work 4 sts in seed st—28 (30, 32, 34) sts rem.

Rows 42–44: Work even in St st and seed st.

Rows 45–50: Work in seed st.

Row 51: (RS; dec row) K2tog, knit to last 4 sts, work 4 sts in seed st—27 (29, 31, 33) sts rem.

Work even in St st and seed st until piece measures 13 (14, 14¼, 15¼)" (33 [35.5, 36, 38.5] cm), ending with a WS row.

Shape armhole

BO 4 sts at beg of next row, then BO 3 sts at beg of foll RS row—20 (22, 24, 26) sts rem.

Dec 1 st at armhole edge every row 3 times, then every other row 0 (1, 2, 3) time(s)—17 (18, 19, 20) sts rem.

Work even until armhole measures 5¾ (5¾, 6½, 6½)" (14.5 [14.5, 16.5, 16.5] cm), ending with a WS row.

Place sts on a holder.

Center Front Panel

With smaller needles, CO 35 (37, 39, 41) sts.

Work in seed st for 10 rows.

Change to larger needles.

Row 11: (RS) Work 4 sts in seed st, k27 (29, 31, 33), work 4 sts in seed st.

Row 12: Work 4 sts in seed st, p27 (29, 31, 33), work 4 sts in seed st.

Rows 13–14: Work even in patt as established.

Row 15: (RS; pattern set-up and buttonhole row) K1, p2tog, yo, p1, k5 (6, 7, 8), pm, work Row 1 of Heart chart, pm, k5 (6, 7, 8), p1, yo, p2tog, k1.

Row 16: Work 4 sts in seed st, purl to m, work Row

2 of Heart chart, p5 (6, 7, 8), work 4 sts in seed st.

Rows 17–28: Work even in patt as established.

Row 29: (RS; buttonhole row) K1, p2tog, yo, p1, knit to m, work Row 15 of Heart chart, k5 (6, 7, 8), p1, yo, p2tog, k1.

Rows 30–40: Work even to end of Heart chart in patt as established, removing markers on last row.

Row 41: (RS) Work 4 sts in seed st, knit to last 4 sts, work 4 sts in seed st.

Row 42: Work 4 sts in seed st, purl to last 4 sts, work 4 sts in seed st.

Row 43: (RS; buttonhole row) K1, p2tog, yo, p1, k27 (29, 31, 33), p1, yo, p2tog, k1.

Row 44: Work 4 sts in seed st, p27 (29, 31, 33), work 4 sts in seed st.

Rows 45–50: Work in seed st.

Row 51: (RS) Work 4 sts in seed st, knit to last 4 sts, work 4 sts in seed st.

Cont in established St st and seed st, placing buttonholes every 14th row (beg counting with last buttonhole worked [Row 43] so that buttonholes are evenly spaced) 4 (4, 4, 5) more times, then work even without buttonholes until piece measures 18¾ (19¾, 20¾, 21¾)" (47.5 [50, 52.5, 55] cm) from CO, ending with a WS row.

Place sts on a holder.

Right Front Panel

With smaller needles, CO 32 (34, 36, 38) sts.

Work in seed st for 10 rows.

Change to larger needles.

Row 1: (RS; dec row) Work 4 sts in seed st, knit to last 2 sts, k2tog—31 (33, 35, 37) sts rem.

Row 12: P27 (29, 31, 33), work 4 sts in seed st.

Row 13: Work 4 sts in seed st, knit to end of row.

Row 14: Purl to last 4 sts, work 4 sts in seed st.

Row 15: (RS; pattern set-up row) Work 4 sts in seed st, k5 (6, 7, 8), pm, work Row 1 of Heart chart, pm, knit to end of row.

Row 16: Purl to m, work Row 2 of Heart chart, purl to last 4 sts, work 4 sts in seed st.

Rows 17–20: Work in St st, seed st, and Heart chart as established.

Heart

	25

(chart rows numbered: 25, 23, 21, 19, 17, 15, 13, 11, 9, 7, 5, 3, 1)

☐ k on RS, p on WS

· p on RS, k on WS

Row 21: (RS; dec row) Work 4 sts in seed st, knit to m, work Row 7 of Heart chart, knit to last 2 sts, k2tog—30 (32, 34, 36) sts rem.

Rows 22–30: Work even in patt as established.

Row 31: (RS; dec row) Work 4 sts in seed st, knit to m, work row 17 of Heart chart, knit to last 2 sts, k2tog—29 (31, 33, 35) sts rem.

Rows 32–40: Work even as established to end of Heart chart, removing markers on last row.

Row 41: (RS; dec row) Work 4 sts in seed st, knit to last 2 sts, k2tog—28 (30, 32, 34) sts rem.

Rows 42–44: Work even in St st and seed st as established.

Rows 45–50: Work in seed st.

Row 51: (RS; dec row) Work 4 sts in seed st, knit to last 2 sts, k2tog—27 (29, 31, 33) sts rem.

Work even in St st and seed st until piece measures 13 (14, 14¼, 15¼)" (33 [35.5, 36, 38.5] cm), ending with a RS row.

Shape armhole

BO 4 sts at beg of next row, then BO 3 sts at beg of foll WS row—20 (22, 24, 26) sts rem.

Dec 1 st at armhole edge every row 3 times, then every other row 0 (1, 2, 3) time(s)—17 (18, 19, 20) sts rem.

Work even until armhole measures 5¾ (5¾, 6½, 6½)" (14.5 [14.5, 16.5, 16.5] cm), ending with a WS row. Place sts on a holder.

Join Panels

Place all held front panel sts on separate needles, using 2 smaller needles and 1 larger needle.

Next row: (RS) With larger needle and RS facing, beg
    with left front panel, work 13 (14, 15, 16) sts in
    seed st. Hold needle with first 4 sts of center front
    panel in front of 4 rem unworked sts of left front
    panel. Work 4 sts in seed st, working first center
    front panel st tog with first rem left front panel st,
    second center front panel st tog with second rem
    left front panel st, and continuing in same manner
    for rem 2 sts—left front panel is joined to center
    front panel. Work 27 (29, 31, 33) center front panel
    sts in seed st. Hold needle with first 4 sts of right
    front panel behind 4 rem unworked sts of center
    front panel. Work 4 sts in seed st, working rem
    center front panel sts tog with right front panel
    sts—center front panel is joined to right front
    panel. Work 13 (14, 15, 16) right front panel sts in
    seed st—61 (65, 69, 73) sts total.
Work 13 rows in seed st.

Shape shoulders and front neck

BO 4 (5, 6, 6) sts, work in seed st until there are 15
(16, 17, 19) sts on right needle. Place rem 42 (44,
46, 48) sts on a holder for right front.
Work both sides of neck separately.
Next row: (WS) BO 3 sts, work in seed st to end of
    row—12 (13, 14, 16) sts rem.
Next row: BO 4 (5, 6, 6) sts, work in seed st to end
    of row—8 (8, 8, 10) sts rem.
Next row: BO 3 sts, work in seed st to end of row—
    5 (5, 5, 7) sts rem.
BO rem 5 (5, 5, 7) sts.
Leave center 23 sts on holder for front neck.

With RS facing, rejoin yarn to rem 19 (21, 23, 25) held sts and work in seed st to end of row.

Next row: (WS) BO 4 (5, 6, 6) sts at beg of row—15 (16, 17, 19) sts rem.

Next row: BO 3 sts, work in seed st to end of row— 12 (13, 14, 16) sts rem.

Next row: BO 4 (5, 6, 6) sts, work in seed st to end of row—8 (8, 8, 10) sts rem.

Next row: BO 3 sts, work in seed st to end of row— 5 (5, 5, 7) sts rem.

BO rem 5 (5, 5, 7) sts.

Sleeves

With smaller needles, CO 41 (41, 43, 43) sts.

Work in Seed st for 12 rows.

Change to larger needles.

*Next row: (RS; inc row) K1, M1 (see Glossary, page 122), knit to last st, M1, k1—2 sts inc'd.

Work 7 rows even in St st.

Rep from * 6 (6, 7, 7) more times—55 (55, 59, 59) sts. Work even until piece measures 14 (14, 15, 15)" (35.5 [35.5, 38, 38] cm) from CO, ending with a WS row.

Shape sleeve cap

BO 4 (4, 5, 5) sts at beg of next 2 rows—47 (47, 49, 49) sts rem.

Dec 1 st each end of needle every row 3 times, then every other row 3 times—35 (35, 37, 37) sts rem.

Work even for 3 rows.

Dec 1 st each end of needle on next row—33 (33, 35, 35) sts rem.

Rep the last 4 rows once more—31 (31, 33, 33) sts rem.

Work 1 WS row even.

Dec 1 st each end of needle every other row 2 times, then every row 3 times—21 (21, 23, 23) sts rem.

BO 3 sts at beg of next 4 rows—9 (9, 11, 11) sts rem. BO rem 9 (9, 11, 11) sts.

Finishing

Block pieces to measurements. With yarn threaded on a tapestry needle, sew front to back at right shoulder.

Neck edging

With smaller needles, RS facing, and beg at left shoulder, pick up and knit 6 sts along left front neck, k23 held front neck sts, pick up and knit 6 sts along right front neck to shoulder, 6 sts along right back neck, k23 held back neck sts, and pick up and knit 6 sts from left back neck to left shoulder—70 sts total.

With WS facing, BO all sts knitwise.

With yarn threaded on a tapestry needle, sew front to back at left shoulder. Sew sleeves into armholes. Sew side and sleeve seams. Weave in loose ends. Block again if desired. Sew buttons onto side panels opposite buttonholes.

Organic Cable Nursing Sweater

Practical and elegant, this sweater demonstrates the essence of this book, taking a simple idea—an organic cable pattern—and crafting a beautiful garment with a purpose: the sweater unbuttons on the left and right for discreet breast-feeding.

To fit bust circumference		
36–38	40–42	44–46"
91.5–96.5	101.5–106.5	112–117 cm
Finished bust circumference		
44	47	50"
112	119.5	127 cm
Actual width at underarm/lower edge		
22	23½	25"
56	59.5	63.5 cm
Armhole depth		
8	8¾	8¾"
20.5	22	22 cm
Neck width		
7	7	7"
18	18	18 cm
Finished length		
22¼	23	23"
56.5	58.5	58.5 cm
Sleeve length to base of cap		
18	19	19"
45.5	48.5	48.5 cm

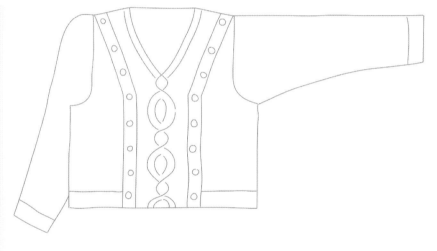

Yarn

Worsted weight (CYCA #4 Medium): 1000 (1105, 1150) yd (914 [1010, 1052] m).

Shown here: Green Mountain Spinnery Green Mountain Green (60% wool, 40% kid mohair; 120 yd [110 m]/2 oz): silver brown, 9 (10, 10) skeins. Sweater shown measures 44" (112 cm).

Needles

U.S. sizes 7 and 8 (4.5 and 5 mm): straight. Adjust needle size if necessary to obtain the correct gauge.

Notions

Cable needle (cn); markers (m); stitch holders; tapestry needle; eighteen ⅝" (1.5-cm) buttons, shown here in mother-of-pearl.

Gauge

16 sts and 22 rows = 4" (10 cm) in St st on larger needles.

Back

With smaller needles, CO 88 (94, 100) sts.
Work in garter st for 10 rows.
Change to larger needles.
Beg with a knit row, work in St st until piece measures 13½" (34.5 cm) from CO, ending with a WS row.

Shape armholes

BO 4 sts at beg of next 2 rows, then BO 3 sts at beg of foll 2 rows—74 (80, 86) sts rem.
Dec 1 st each end of needle every row 3 times, then every other row 1 (2, 3) time(s)—66 (70, 74) sts rem.
Work even until armhole measures 8 (8¾, 8¾)" (20.5 [22, 22] cm), ending with a WS row.

Shape shoulders and back neck

BO 5 (6, 7) sts at beg of next 2 rows—56 (58, 60) sts rem.
BO 5 (6, 7) sts at beg of foll row, knit until there are 9 sts on right needle, turn. Place rem 42 (43, 44) sts on a holder for left back.
Work right side of neck separately.
Next row: BO 3 sts, purl to end—6 sts rem.
BO rem 6 sts.
Leave center 28 sts on holder for back neck. With RS facing, rejoin yarn to rem 14 (15, 16) held left back sts, knit to end.
BO 5 (6, 7) sts, purl to end—9 sts rem.
Next row: BO 3 sts, knit to end—6 sts rem.
BO rem 6 sts.

Front

Left front panel

With smaller needles, CO 34 (37, 40) sts.
Work in garter st for 10 rows. Change to larger needles.
Row 11: (RS) Knit.
Row 12: K4, purl to end.
Rep these 2 rows 32 more times—piece measures about 13½" (34.5 cm) from CO. Place sts on a holder.

Center front panel

With smaller needles, CO 24 sts.
Foundation row: (WS; inc row) K7, M1 (see Glossary, page 122), k2, M1, k6, M1, k2, M1, k7—28 sts.
Row 1: (RS) Knit.
Row 2: K7, p4, k6, p4, k7.
Rep Rows 1–2 eight more times. Change to larger needles.
Work Rows 1–66 of Cable chart, working Rows 7–30 two times. (Last 2 rows of chart will be worked later.) Piece measures about 13½" (34.5 cm) from CO.
Place sts on a holder.

Right front panel

With smaller needles, CO 34 (37, 40) sts.
Work in garter st for 10 rows.
Change to larger needles.
Row 11: (RS) Knit.
Row 12: Purl to last 4 sts, k4.
Rep these 2 rows 32 more times—piece measures about 13½" (34.5 cm) from CO. Place sts on a holder.

Join panels

Place held front panel sts onto separate needles, using 2 smaller needles and 1 larger needle.
Next row: With RS facing, a larger needle, and beg with left front panel, k30 (33, 36) sts. Hold needle

Cable

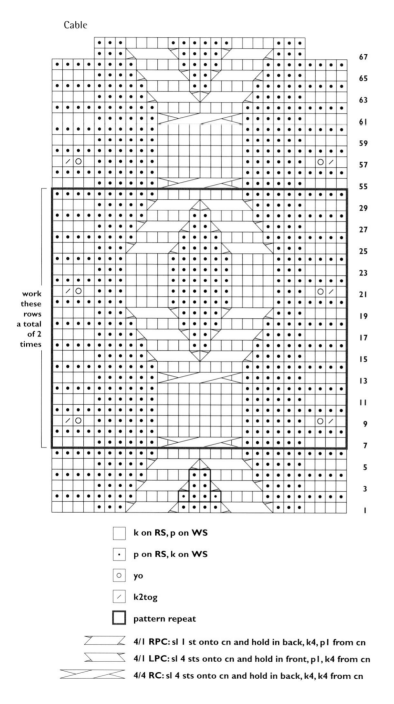

k on RS, p on WS

· p on RS, k on WS

○ yo

╱ k2tog

pattern repeat

4/1 **RPC:** sl 1 st onto cn and hold in back, k4, p1 from cn

4/1 **LPC:** sl 4 sts onto cn and hold in front, p1, k4 from cn

4/4 **RC:** sl 4 sts onto cn and hold in back, k4, k4 from cn

with first 4 sts of center front panel in front of 4 rem unworked sts of left front panel. Join panels by knitting first center front panel st tog with first rem left front panel st, second center front panel st tog with second rem left front panel st, and cont in same manner for rem 2 sts.

Work Row 67 of Cable chart across 20 sts of center front panel. Hold needle with first 4 sts of right front panel behind 4 rem unworked sts of center front panel. Join panels by knitting next 4 sts of center front panel tog with first 4 sts of right front panel, k30 (33, 36) right front panel sts—88 (94, 100) sts total.

Next row: P30 (33, 36), k4, work Row 68 of Cable chart, k4, p30 (33, 36).

Shape armhole and left front neck

Row 1: (RS) BO 4 sts, knit until there are 24 (27, 30) sts on right needle, k2tog, place marker (pm), k4, p3, k7, turn—39 (42, 45) sts. Place rem 44 (47, 50) sts on a holder for right front. Work left side of neck separately.

Row 2: K3, p4, k7, p25 (28, 31).

Row 3: BO 3 sts, knit to 2 sts before m, k2tog, sl m, k4, p3, k7—35 (38, 41) sts rem.

Row 4: K3, p4, k7, purl to end of row.

Dec 1 st at armhole edge every row 3 times, then every other row 1 (2, 3) time(s), and *at the same time* cont to dec for neck before m as established every other row 11 times, then every 4th row 4 times—16 (18, 20) sts rem.

Work even until armhole measures 8 (8³/₄, 8³/₄)" (20.5 [22, 22] cm), ending with a WS row.

BO 5 (6, 7) sts at beg of next RS row 2 times—6 sts rem.
Work 1 row even.
BO rem 6 sts.

Shape armhole and right front neck

With RS facing, rejoin yarn to 44 (47, 50) held right front sts.

Row 1: (RS) K7, p3, k4, pm, ssk, knit to end of row—43 (46, 49) sts rem.

Row 2: BO 4 sts, purl to m, k7, p4, k3—39 (42, 45) sts rem.

Row 3: K7, p3, k4, sl m, ssk, knit to end of row—38 (41, 44) sts rem.

Row 4: BO 3 sts, purl to m, k7, p4, k3—35 (38, 41) sts rem.

Dec 1 st at armhole edge every row 3 times, then every other row 1 (2, 3) time(s), and *at the same time* cont to dec for neck after m as established every other row 11 times, then every 4th row 4 times—16 (18, 20) sts rem.

Work even until armhole measures 8 (8¾, 8¾)" (20.5 [22, 22] cm), ending with a RS row.
BO 5 (6, 7) sts at beg of next WS row 2 times—6 sts rem.
Work 1 row even.
BO rem 6 sts.

Sleeves

With smaller needles, CO 42 (44, 44) sts.
Work in garter st for 12 rows.
Change to larger needles.

Next row: (RS; inc row) K1, M1, knit to last st, M1, k1—2 sts inc'd.

Work 13 (11, 11) rows even in St st. Rep last 14 (12, 12) rows 5 (6, 6) more times, then work inc row once more—56 (60, 60) sts.

Work even until piece measures 18 (19, 19)" (45.5 [48.5, 48.5] cm) from CO, ending with a WS row.

Shape sleeve cap

BO 4 (5, 5) sts at beg of next 2 rows—48 (50, 50) sts rem.

Dec 1 st each end of needle every row 3 times, then every other row 3 times—36 (38, 38) sts rem.

Dec 1 st each end of needle every 4th row 2 times—32 (34, 34) sts rem.

Dec 1 st each end of needle every other row 2 times, then every row 3 times—22 (24, 24) sts rem.

BO 3 sts at beg of next 4 rows—10 (12, 12) sts rem.
BO rem 10 (12, 12) sts.

Finishing

Block pieces to measurements.

Back neck edging

With smaller needles, RS facing, and beg at right shoulder, pick up and knit 3 sts from shoulder to back neck holder, k28 held back neck sts, and pick up and knit 3 sts to shoulder—34 sts total.

With WS facing, BO all sts knitwise.

With yarn threaded on a tapestry needle, sew shoulder seams. Sew sleeves into armholes. Sew side and sleeve seams. Weave in loose ends. Block again if desired.

Sew buttons onto left and right front panels opposite buttonholes on center front panel. Sew on buttons as decoration around V neck edge as shown in photograph.

Leafy Lace Shawl

This wonderful nursing shawl is worked in an easy lace stitch with a fabulously soft chunky yarn. When it comes time to feed your baby, night or day, throw on this shawl and feel enveloped in love and warmth, experiencing the joy that nursing your new baby brings.

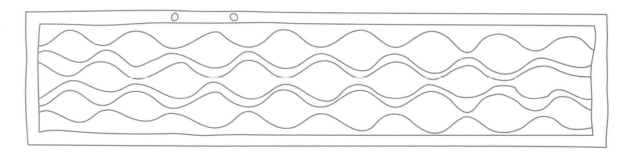

Finished width
16"   40.5 cm
Finished length
60"   152.5 cm

Yarn
Bulky weight (CYCA Super Bulky #6): 415 yd (379m).
Shown here: Vreseis Fox Fibre Boiled Cotton Chenille (100% Colorganic cotton; 600 yd [549 m]/lb: green, 11 oz (308 g). *Note:* Yarn is available in 3–5 oz (85–140 g) skeins.
Needles
U.S. size 15 (10 mm): straight. Adjust needle size if necessary to obtain the correct gauge.

Notions
Two 1¼" (3.2-cm) buttons (optional), shown here in mother-of-pearl; sewing needle; matching sewing thread or fine yarn for attaching buttons.
Gauge
8½ sts and 12 rows = 4" (10 cm) in lace patt.

Shawl
CO 35 sts.
Work 2 rows in garter st.
Rows 1, 3, and 5: (RS) K2, [k1, yo, k3, sl1, k2tog, psso, k3, yo] 3 times, k3.
Row 2 and all even (WS) rows: K2, p31, k2.
Rows 7, 9, and 11: K2, k2tog, [k3, yo, k1, yo, k3, sl1,

k2tog, psso] twice, k3, yo, k1, yo, k3, ssk, k2.

Row 12: K2, p31, k2.

Rep Rows 1–12 thirteen more times, then work Rows 1–11 once more, ending with a RS row.

Work 2 rows in garter stitch. With WS facing, BO all sts knitwise.

Finishing

With sewing needle and thread or fine yarn, sew buttons onto right edge of piece about 14" (35.5 cm) and 16" (40.5 cm) from CO edge. Use large eyelet holes in shawl opposite buttons as buttonholes.

Abbreviations

beg	beginning; begin; begins		psso	pass slipped stitch over
BO	bind off		pwise	purlwise, as if to purl
CC	contrast color		rem	remain(s); remaining
cm	centimeter(s)		rep	repeat(s)
cn	cable needle		rnd(s)	round(s)
CO	cast on		RS	right side
cont	continue(s); continuing		sl	slip
dec(s)	decrease(s); decreasing		sl st	slip stitch (slip 1 stitch pwise unless otherwise indicated)
foll	following; follows			
g	gram(s)		ssk	slip 2 sts kwise, one at a time, from the left needle to right needle, insert left needle tip through both front loops and knit together from this position (1 st decrease)
inc(s)	increase(s); increasing			
k	knit			
k1f&b	knit into the front and back of same stitch			
k2tog	knit two stitches together		St st	stockinette stitch
k3tog	knit three stitches together		st(s)	stitch(es)
kwise	knitwise, as if to knit		tbl	through back loop
lb	pound		tog	together
m	marker(s)		WS	wrong side
MC	main color		wyb	with yarn in back
mm	millimeter(s)		wyf	with yarn in front
M1	make one (increase)		yd	yard(s)
oz	ounce(s)		yo	yarnover
p	purl		*	repeat starting point
p1f&b	purl into front and back of same stitch		( )	alternate measurements and/or instructions
p2tog	purl two stitches together		[ ]	instructions are worked as a group a specified number of times
patt(s)	pattern(s)			

Glossary of Terms and Techniques

BIND-OFFS
Standard Bind-Off

Knit the first stitch, *knit the next stitch (2 stitches on right needle), insert left needle tip into first stitch on right needle (Figure 1) and lift this stitch up and over the second stitch (Figure 2) and off the needle (Figure 3). Repeat from * for the desired number of stitches. If you find that the bound-off edge is too tight, try binding off with a larger needle than the one with which the piece was knitted.

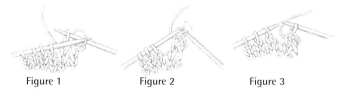

Figure 1   Figure 2   Figure 3

Three-Needle Bind-Off

Place stitches to be joined onto two separate needles. Hold the needles parallel. Insert a third needle into first stitch on each of the other two needles (Figure 1) and knit them together (Figure 2), *knit the next stitch on each needle together in the same way, then pass the first stitch over the second (Figure 3). Repeat from * until one stitch remains on third needle. Cut yarn and pull tail through the last stitch.

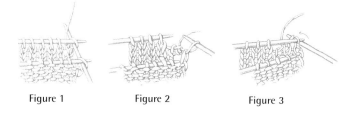

Figure 1   Figure 2   Figure 3

BLOCKING
Pressing

Pressing the knitted fabric will help the pieces maintain their shape and give them a smooth finish. With the wrong side of the fabric facing, pin each knitted piece to the measurements given onto an ironing board. As each yarn is different, refer to the ball band and press pieces according to instructions.

CAST-ONS
Cable Cast-On

Make a slipknot and place it on the left needle for the first stitch. Insert the right needle into the stitch and knit it, but don't drop the old stitch from the left needle. Place the new stitch on the left needle. *Insert right needle between the first two stitches on left needle (Figure 1), wrap yarn around needle as if to knit, draw yarn through (Figure 2), and place new loop on left needle (Figure 3) to form a new stitch. Repeat from * for the desired number of stitches, always working between the first two stitches on the left needle.

Figure 1   Figure 2   Figure 3

Long-Tail Cast-On

Leaving a long tail (about ½" [1.3 cm] for each stitch to be cast on), make a slipknot and place on right needle. Place thumb and index finger of your left hand between the yarn ends so that working yarn is around your index finger and tail end is around your thumb. Secure the yarn ends with your other fingers and hold your palm upwards, making a V of yarn (Figure 1). *Bring needle up through loop on thumb (Figure 2), catch first strand around index finger, and go back down through loop on thumb (Figure 3). Drop loop off thumb and, placing thumb back in V configuration, tighten resulting stitch on needle (Figure 4). Repeat from * for the desired number of stitches.

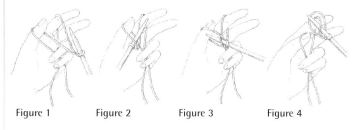

Figure 1   Figure 2   Figure 3   Figure 4

CHARTS

The instructions for several patterns in this book use both written and visual instructions—charts. We use charts when writing out the whole pattern would be very complicated. Once you begin to visualize your knitting in relation to the chart, it becomes easier to be creative with your knitting, as you can treat the knitted fabric as a picture and "paint" with texture and color.

A chart represents each stitch as a box on a sheet of graph paper; each square represents one stitch, and each line of squares designates a row of knitting. The chart's symbols indicate how to work each stitch.

Reading the chart is easier if you visualize it as the right side of a piece of knitting, working from the lower edge to the top. When knitting back and forth, read right-side rows (which are usually odd-numbered rows) from right to left and wrong-side rows (even-numbered) from left to right. If you're knitting in the round, read every row from right to left.

CROCHET CHAIN

Make a slipknot and place on crochet hook. *Yarn over hook and draw it through loop on hook. Repeat from * for desired length. To fasten off, cut yarn and draw tail through last loop formed.

DECREASES
K2tog

Knit 2 stitches together as if they were a single stitch.

Ssk

Slip 2 stitches individually knitwise (Figure 1), insert left needle tip into the front of these 2 slipped stitches, and use the right needle to knit them together through their back loops (Figure 2).

Figure 1   Figure 2

P2tog

Purl 2 stitches together as if they were a single stitch.

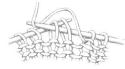

EMBELLISHMENTS
Lazy Daisy Stitch

With yarn threaded on a tapestry needle, bring the needle out from back to front at the center of a knitted stitch. *Form a short loop and insert needle back where it came out. Bring the needle from back to front inside the formed loop and pass it to the back outside the loop, securing the loop to the knitted fabric (Figure 1). Beginning each stitch at the same point on the knitted background, repeat from * several times to form a flower (Figure 2), or work singly to create a leaf. Lazy daisy stitch looks effective as self-colored embroidery or in contrast colors, using up remnants of yarn.

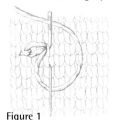

Figure 1   Figure 2

French Knots

With yarn threaded on a tapestry needle, bring the needle from the back to the front of the work and wind the yarn several times around the needle according to the size of knot required. Take the needle back near where it came out and draw the yarn through, forming a small knot on the right side of work.

Pom-poms

Used for the rabbit's "cotton" tail. Cut two circles of cardboard, each slightly bigger than the size of the desired pom-pom. Cut a smaller hole in the center of each circle, about half the size of the original diameter—the larger this hole is, the fuller the pom-pom (Figure 1). Holding the two circles together, wind several strands of yarn through the ring until it is completely covered. (As the hole at the center fills up, you may find it easier to use a darning needle to pass the yarn through.) Cut between the two circles using a pair of sharp scissors, making sure all the yarn has been cut (Figure 2). Separate the two circles slightly, wrap a strand of yarn between them, and knot firmly (Figure 3). Pull the two circles apart and fluff the pom-pom to cover the tie. Trim the pom-pom if necessary, but don't get carried away.

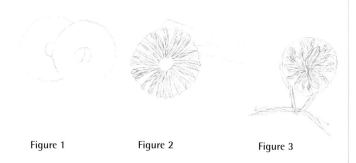

Figure 1   Figure 2   Figure 3

Twisted Cord

Used to fasten the boy's booties and join the mittens for older babies. Cut two lengths of yarn as specified in pattern. Knot the strands together at each end. Attach one end to a hook or door handle and insert a knitting needle through the other end. Twist the strands together (Figure 1); the tighter the twist, the firmer the finished cord will be. Holding the cord in the center with one hand (you may need some help), bring both ends of cord together, allowing the two halves to twist together (Figure 2). Keep the cord straight and avoid tangling. Knot the cut ends together and trim.

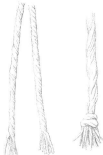

Figure 1   Figure 2

GARTER STITCH

Garter stitch produces a reversible textured fabric that is very elastic lengthwise. When working back and forth to produce flat pieces, knit every stitch of every row. When working circularly, alternate rows of all knit and all purl.

GAUGE

Gauge is an indispensable part of any knitting pattern. Each pattern is worked out mathematically, and if the correct gauge is not achieved, the project will not fit as intended. Before embarking on knitting your garment, we recommend you check your gauge. Using the recommended needle size, cast on 30 to 40 stitches and, in the pattern stitch specified in the instructions, work at least 4" (10 cm) from the cast-on edge. Remove the stitches from the needle or bind off loosely and lay the swatch on a flat surface. Place a ruler or tape measure across it and, in the space of 4" (10 cm), count the number of stitches across and rows down (including fractions of stitches and rows). Repeat this measurement in two or three places on the swatch to confirm your initial measurement. If you have more stitches and rows than called for in the pattern's instructions, try again using larger needles; if you have too few stitches or rows, try again with smaller needles. *Note:* Check your gauge regularly as you knit, as it can become tighter or looser as you become relaxed and confident with your knitting.

Some of the patterns include ribs, textured patterns, or cables, which can change the gauge substantially. The pattern will specify whether the gauge swatch should be worked in stockinette or another stitch.

INCREASES

K1f&b

Knit into a stitch but leave it on the left needle (Figure 1), then knit through the back loop of the same stitch (Figure 2) and slip the original stitch off the needle.

| Figure 1 | Figure 2 |

Make One (M1)

With left needle tip, lift the strand between last knitted stitch and first stitch on left needle from back to front (Figure 1), then knit the lifted strand through the front loop (Figure 2).

Figure 1   Figure 2

Yarnover Increase (yo)

Wrap the working yarn around the needle from front to back, then bring yarn into position to work the next stitch (leave it in back if a knit stitch follows; bring it under the needle to the front if a purl stitch follows).

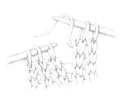

LACE KNITTING

The lace patterns in this book use yarnovers to create eyelets. Each yarnover usually corresponds to a decrease, so that the number of stitches remains constant at the end of each row. Some patterns are achieved by increasing stitches on some rows and decreasing them on subsequent rows. Although these patterns are quite complex, the effect is very rewarding.

PICK UP AND KNIT

Work from right to left with right side facing. For horizontal (bind-off or cast-on) edges: Insert tip of needle into the center of the stitch below the bind-off or cast-on edge (Figure 1), wrap yarn around needle, and pull it through to make a stitch on the needle (Figure 2). Pick up one stitch for every stitch along the horizontal edge. For shaped edges, insert needle between last and second-to-last stitches, wrap yarn around needle, and pull it through to make a stitch on the needle (Figure 3). Pick up about three stitches for every four rows along the shaped edge.

Figure 1   Figure 2   Figure 3

SEAMS

Backstitch Seam

With right sides together, pin the pieces to be joined together so that their edges are even. Insert the threaded needle from back to front through both pieces at the right-hand edge, take the yarn around the edges and reinsert the yarn through the same stitch, pulling tight to secure. *Insert the needle from back to front two stitches to the left (Figure 1), then from front to back one stitch to the right (Figure 2). Repeat from * to the end, pull the yarn firmly, and fasten off on the wrong side.

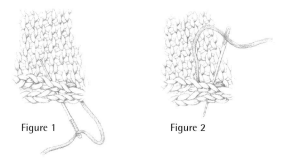

Figure 1   Figure 2

Edge to Edge Stitch

This method produces a seam that is nearly invisible from both the right and wrong sides of the fabric. With wrong sides facing up and the edges to be joined lying edge to edge, insert a threaded tapestry needle through the knot formed by a purl stitch on one piece, then through the corresponding knot on the second piece. *Insert the needle through the next stitch on the first piece and the next stitch on the second piece. Working back and forth between the two pieces, repeat from * to the end, pull the yarn firmly, and fasten off on the inside.

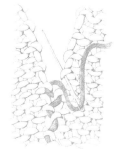

Mattress Stitch

This seam, worked on the right side of the fabric, is ideal for matching stripes. Mattress stitch should be worked one stitch in from the edge to give the best finish. With the right sides facing and the two pieces to be joined lying edge to edge, use a threaded tapestry needle to pick up one bar between the first two stitches on one piece (Figure 1). Take the needle to the front of the opposite piece and lift the corresponding bar plus the bar above it (Figure 2). *Pick up the next two bars on the first piece, then the next two bars on the other (Figure 3). Repeat from * to the end, pulling the yarn in the direction of the seam. Finish by picking up the last bar or pair of bars at the top of the first piece. Pull the yarn firmly and fasten off inside.

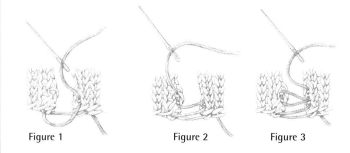

Figure 1   Figure 2   Figure 3

Whipstitch

With right sides facing up and the two pieces to be joined lying edge to edge, insert a threaded tapestry needle from front to back through one stitch at the edge of one piece, then bring the needle back up through the corresponding stitch on the other piece. *Insert the needle from front to back in the next stitch on the first piece and bring the needle from back to front in the corresponding stitch on the second piece. Working in a circular motion, repeat from * to the end, pulling the yarn in the direction of the seam. Pull the yarn firmly and fasten off inside.

SHORT-ROWS

Work to turning point, slip next stitch purlwise to right needle, then bring the yarn to the front (Figure 1). Slip the same stitch back to the left needle (Figure 2), turn the work around and bring the yarn in position for the next stitch, wrapping the slipped stitch with working yarn as you do so. When you come to a wrapped stitch on a subsequent row, hide the wrap by working it together with the wrapped stitch as follows: Insert right needle tip under the wrap (from the front if wrapped stitch is a knit stitch; from the back if wrapped stitch is a purl stitch), then into the stitch on the needle, and work the stitch and its wrap together as a single stitch.

Figure 1   Figure 2

WEAVING IN ENDS

Once you have blocked your finished pieces, weave in all loose ends. Using a tapestry needle, weave each loose end through about five stitches on the wrong side of the fabric, then pull the end through and trim it close. Do not weave two ends in the same area.

Many knitters find this a very tedious task, but it is well worth putting in the effort. Sew in all ends—don't be tempted to use a long yarn end for sewing up. Use a separate length of yarn to sew pieces together, so that you can undo the seam if necessary without the danger of unraveling your knitting.

Figure 1   Figure 2

Yarn suppliers

I would like to thank the yarn suppliers for their kind sponsorship.
Their yarns inspired me to create the beautiful designs in this book.

Cottage Industry
409 South Division Street
Northfield, MN 55057
(507) 664-3870
www.cottageindustry.net

Blue Sky Alpacas
PO Box 387
St. Francis, MN 55070
(763) 753-5815 or (888) 460-8862
www.blueskyalpacas.com

Green Mountain Spinnery
PO Box 568
Putney, VT 05346
(802) 387-4528
spinnery@sover.net
www.spinnery.com

Vreseis Limited
PO Box 69
Guinda, CA 95637
530-796-3007
info@vreseis.com
www.vreseis.com

Garthenor Organic Pure Wool
Llanio Road
Tregaron, Wales SY25 6UR
United Kingdom
+44 1570 493 347
garthenor@organicpurewool.co.uk
www.organicpurewool.co.uk

Index